DESIGNING GAMES FOR CHILDREN

DESIGNING GAMES FOR CHILDREN

Developmental, Usability, and Design Considerations for Making Games for Kids

Carla Fisher, Ed.D.

Routledge
Taylor & Francis Group
New York London

First published 2015
by Focal Press

711 Third Avenue, New York, NY 10017, USA
2 Park Square, Milton Park, Abingdon, Oxon OX14 4RN

Routledge is an imprint of the Taylor & Francis Group, an informa business

First issued in hardback 2017

Practitioners and researchers must always rely on their own experience and knowledge in evaluating and using any information, methods, compounds, or experiments described herein. In using such information or methods they should be mindful of their own safety and the safety of others, including parties for whom they have a professional responsibility.

Library of Congress Cataloging-in-Publication Data
CIP data has been applied for

ISBN: 978-0-415-72917-8 (pbk)
ISBN: 978-1-138-42829-4 (hbk)

Typeset in Minion Pro
by Apex CoVantage, LLC

For Lo and all the budding gamers just like you.

Contents

Acknowledgments

Thanks to Sean Connelly for making this book happen. And great thanks to Caitlin Murphy for patiently ushering me through the process and for making sure I actually finished the book. Now I've confirmed that I'm hard-nosed on all deadlines except my own self-imposed ones.

Many, many colleagues have helped me gnaw on the various topics addressed in this book. It's impossible to thank them all by name, but suffice it to say that if their game is mentioned in this book, it's because I admire the contribution they've made to our industry.

I also underestimated the challenge of using a bunch of words to describe something as dynamic as games. So my extreme gratitude to all who provide permission to show images of their games. The good people of the world who have released images under Creative Commons Attribution License on Flickr also made this a much prettier book.

Thanks, Anne Richards, for years of designing, friendship, and spirited feedback. Had you not been a part of this extended journey, my arguments would be fuzzy and there'd be a lot of improper grammar going on.

I also owe my longtime friend and colleague Silvia Lovato for your great suggestions as the manuscript came together. Thanks, too, to Barbara Chamberlin for your comments. Arielle Martinez and Katie Ostroth were instrumental in providing much-needed editorial support.

My colleagues at Kidscreen who have supported the Kids Got Game blog also have my sincere gratitude, particularly Lana Castleman, as much of the foundation of this book was laid in that blog.

Finally, thank you, Jonathan, for finding a way to keep the world revolving smoothly when I accepted one more project, one more conference, one more game, and one wee book. In the future, I promise we won't move cross-country at the same time the final manuscript is due.

About the Author

Dr. Carla Fisher specializes in creating thoughtful and age-appropriate interactive education and entertainment for children and families. In 2010 she founded No Crusts Interactive, a studio focused on educational game design and interactive media consulting, and she has previously worked for Sesame Workshop, PBS KIDS, and Highlights for Children.

Over the past 15 years, she's had a hand in creating and researching more than 300 games for all kinds of technology platforms and numerous beloved children's brands. Through No Crusts, she and her team designed Kids' CBC *Little Wally Ball-y Ball* (iOS) for *Monster Math Squad*/DHX, which was selected as Apple New & Noteworthy as well as being featured as one of the 10 best Canadian-made games of 2013. (Dr. Fisher is American. Ask for the story.) They also designed several titles for Warner Bros. Interactive Entertainment, including *Sesame Street: Elmo's Musical Monsterpiece* (Nintendo Wii), which *Entertainment Weekly* called "perfect for budding Beethovens."

Her independent game *Stride & Prejudice* (iOS and Kindle Fire), an endless runner played on the text of *Pride and Prejudice*, reached #7 in the U.S. Apple Education category and was reviewed in numerous press outlets around the world. She also independently produced *Williamspurrrrg HD: A Game of Cat and Mustache* (iPad), which is regularly featured by Apple in the Best Games for Children Ages 9–11 category.

Because she has firsthand experience translating research and developmental psychology into actionable design guidelines, Dr. Fisher is an active contributor to the information available to children's media developers. Her articles and lectures on best practices have reached tens of thousands of media creators in dozens of countries over the past five years. She is a frequent contributor to the Kids Got Game blog on Kidscreen, which she cofounded with Anne Richards in 2011.

Introduction

Designing games for children demands developmentally appropriate game design. In other words, the games have to be designed for the child. But, as adults, we're far removed from the hallmark experiences of childhood, even though we were children once upon a time. We simply don't remember what it's like to not automatically know how to read the squiggles on a piece of paper, nor do we remember the struggle to learn to throw a ball or ride a bicycle. As parents, aunts, uncles, cousins, and friends of those with children, we witness the stages of development once again. As designers, we must not only see what it's like to be a child but also internalize how to design for their specific needs, be it cognitive, physical, social, or emotional.

I've been making educational digital media products for kids for 15 years. I've worked with many beloved brands, including Sesame Street, Highlights for Children, and PBS KIDS, and designed on topics ranging from letters to numbers to dog breeding genetics to sneeze hygiene. Even so, I'm always learning how to design better, particularly for kids.

My approach to design as well as this book have evolved from my work as a game designer, user researcher, and lecturer in games. My goal was less about creating a how-to manual for making kids' games and more about creating a guide to understanding the qualities that make games for children good—be it from a usability, cognitive, physical, or social angle.

About This Book

On the basis of my past experiences, I think it's a fair assumption that anyone reading this book is from one of three groups:

- Game design professionals who have knowledge of the design process but need additional information on how the process or content differs for children.
- Children's media industry professionals or researchers who have knowledge of the children's market but are not as familiar with how to make interactive content for kids. Often these are intellectual property holders who want to extend their brand into games.
- Enterprising and motivated n00bs (pronounced "noob"—gamer-speak for newbie)—who see an opportunity to make games for kids but are unfamiliar with the entire process.

Designing Games for Children is written with these three audiences in mind.

Section One is an overview of game design, including types of games, as well as the process (documentation, roles), and the common business models. It provides the basic tools and vocabulary that a designer needs. Game design professionals may prefer to skim this section.

Section Two is all about kids, including what kids are able to do at various ages (including preschool, early elementary, and tweens). It also includes information on user testing with kids and a discussion of societal concerns about games and kids. Children's-media professionals may want to skim this section.

Section Three is for everyone—it includes the design guidelines, with topics including interaction design, tutorials, e-books, and cooperative gameplay. Since marketing is often an afterthought (though I strongly believe it should begin during development), a chapter on marketing games is also included in this section.

The last section is a brief recap of how to bring together the resources in this book. The appendix includes additional resources for learning more about game design and/or children.

Limitations

I learned while writing my dissertation that noting the limitations in advance is actually a helpful tool for readers. So, with that in mind, here are a few limitations of this text.

1. The focus of this book is children ages 2–12. Babies and toddlers (kids under 2) and teens are briefly discussed to provide the full developmental psychology picture.
2. In general, you'll likely notice a tendency toward educational games. This is because the majority of content created for kids is educational, as opposed to commercial. It's not required to make explicitly educational games, particularly for older children.
3. Similarly, the guidelines and games discussed are generally focused on games that are used in home. Games that are designed explicitly for educational settings are discussed, but the emphasis is on informal game use.

4. This is written largely to be platform-agnostic. In other words, almost all of the guidelines can be applied to any device. Where the information is targeted to a specific platform or interaction, that is noted. Examples are largely focused on mobile, particularly Apple iOS, platforms, because that is where the majority of children's development currently happens.

5. An overview of games production is included, particularly in Section One. This is not an exhaustive explanation. While design methodologies are addressed as part of the discussion, the focus is on children's developmental needs. In this sense, *Designing Games for Children* should be used in conjunction with general game design books.

Play On

I'm going to stand on my soapbox for a moment: The best thing you can do to make great games is to play a lot of them and watch kids play a lot of games. Reading about games and kids will get you pretty far, but nothing compares to that actual experience.

To the first point of playing games, I've provided examples of games to illustrate as many points as possible. Whenever possible, please play those games to fully understand the discussion.

To the point of watching kids play, you'll notice that I frequently mention user testing. It's really that important. But you can also gather information informally by watching kids in everyday life. (Though make sure you're not doing it in a potentially creepy way!)

As I live by user testing, please let me know your thoughts and how you've used the book. Happy designing!

Blue skies,
Carla Fisher
Carla.C.Fisher@gmail.com

PART 1

Game Design in a Nutshell

Image used under Creative Commons Attribution License by Flickr member Neeta Lind.

This section is for those who are new to game design, including those who are experienced children's media producers looking to grow their brand into interactive games. While entire volumes are written on game design and production processes, this section is meant to familiarize readers with the basic tools, vocabulary, and stages of creating a game. This is by no means an exhaustive review of everything involved in the production of a game, but it's as much as I could reasonably fit! Topics covered include game design documents, game production processes, common roles on the production team, and an overview of business models, budgets, and publishing options for children's games.

CHAPTER 1
What Is a Game?

Defining exactly what makes a game is the subject of much heated debate. This chapter attempts to provide a working answer to the question "What is a game?"

Topics to be discussed include:
- An overview of the basic goals and features of a game
- Genres of games
- Various distribution platforms for games

Games Can Be Many Things

For every person you ask, "What is a game?" you will get a different answer. It has a wide range of definitions, but for our purposes of focusing on children's games, a game is an interactive experience, where one or more players are presented a goal and has to take action to reach that goal. A set of rules constrains the ways in which the player can reach the goal. The player often has to overcome obstacles to reach the goal, as well.

Tic-Tac-Toe is a game where players take turn placing their icon on a board until one player gets three in a row.

Tetris is a game where the player places blocks in various shapes onto a grid. When a horizontal line is completely filled in, the line is cleared. The game continues until the board is filled with incomplete horizontal lines. For every 10 lines that the player clears, the shapes fall a little quicker.

The goal of *Scribblenauts* (Nintendo DS, iOS, and numerous other platforms) is to help the character get the starite. The player types words into a giant word bank to get objects. Then the character uses the object to get the starite. So the character might climb a ladder to reach the starite in the tree.

From there, game designers can add numerous layers to make puzzles that range from simple to incredibly complex.

Games have multiple ways of designating the audience, including:
- Casual—a player who tends to have limited time to play. Casual games are often designed to be played in short bursts.
- Core or midcore—a player who enjoys a wide range of games but will invest time to play games that require a larger time commitment to complete.
- Hardcore—a player who invests a lot of time and energy in playing, often by playing games that require dozens of hours to complete. Hardcore gamers are often considered the stereotypical gamer.

In addition, games can be identified as serious games or educational games. Serious games are ones that have a learning or prosocial benefit, such as training simulations or games that raise awareness for a topic, such as HIV or domestic violence. Serious games are created for all ages, from kids to senior citizens, on a huge range of subjects, from sex education to military training. By definition, educational games for kids are serious games, but they are rarely referred to as serious games. Rather, they are referred to as children's educational games.

It's not uncommon to find entertainment games that have educational extensions that were not expressly designed as educational. Games that are commercial in nature but can be used in education are referred to as "commercial off the shelf" (COTS). For example, even though *Scribblenauts* is an entertainment game, it can also be used educationally for vocabulary development.

Game Genres

Just like films or books, games are identified by genres, which are generally defined by the style of interaction. Like the actual definition of a game, the taxonomy of game genres is debated. It also evolves quickly.

What follows are common game genres, but this is by no means an exhaustive list. Note that these genres cover all games, not just those for children. Genres are not mutually exclusive; many can be combined. Just about any genre can be designed with content and interactions that make it an educational game.

Maze

In the simplest form, a game in the maze genre presents the challenge to navigate from point A to point B. *Pac-Man* is a maze game in which you also avoid enemies and collect items.

Platform

Sometimes referred to as platformers, games in the platformer genre involve traveling from point to point (often platform to platform) by running, jumping, or other actions. The Nintendo franchise *Super Mario Bros.* is one of the best-known platformers.

First Person Shooter

These games, often abbreviated FPS, are a subgenre of shooter games. Shooter games are combat games involving projectiles (most commonly bullets of some sort, but other, less violent objects can also be used). "First Person Shooter" refers to a camera angle where the player is viewing the game as though they are actually the shooter, as opposed to "Third Person Shooter" where the player sees the entire body and weapon of the character he is controlling. *Halo* and *Call of Duty* are well-known FPS games.

Shoot 'em Up

Another subgenre of the shooter category, this one focuses on shooting a lot of enemies while avoiding enemy fire. *Space Invaders* is a classic shoot-'em-up game.

Puzzle

Puzzle games require the player to perform actions to solve a challenge. *Tetris*, *Peggle*, *Bejeweled*, and *Candy Crush Saga* are all puzzle games. The latter two are the Match-3 style of puzzle game, where the user has to match particular tiles to progress. Hidden-Object-Games (HOGs) are also puzzle games, where the user locates items hidden within a picture.

Physics-Based

Physics-based games are often puzzle games, where the player has to perform an action to solve a particular challenge. *Angry Birds* is the most classic example. In the game, one or more aspects of physics are modeled and become the core interaction of the game. In *Angry Birds*, the player uses a slingshot to fling birds toward a structure with the goal of knocking down the structure. The angle of release, the distance sling shot is pulled, and the size of the bird all impact the outcome. *World of Goo* is another well-known physics-based puzzle game.

Adventure

Adventure games involve solving lots of puzzles, often by navigating around a world and interacting with characters. The early adventure games, including *Colossal Cave Adventure* in the 1970s, were text adventures or interactive fiction, such as *Zork* or *Hitchhiker's Guide to the Galaxy*. These were entirely text-based games, where the player read descriptions and controlled the character by typing "Go North" or "Examine Mailbox."

As computing power and development environments improved, the adventure genre gave way to graphic adventure games, including

King's Quest, Leisure Suit Larry, and *Myst.* To navigate the world, the user points the mouse to a location and then clicks the mouse to move a character to the location, leading to the name "point-and-click adventure."

While they are nowhere near the level of popularity they had the 1980s, the adventure genre continues. One of the most notable of the past few years is *The Walking Dead* video game, created by Telltale Games for the television show of the same name.

Role Playing

Digital role-playing games (RPGs) evolved from pen-and-paper-based role-playing games such as *Dungeons & Dragons.* In the digital versions, the player takes on a character that has special skills and abilities. Through quests and challenges, the player earns experience points and levels up the abilities of the character. Well-known RPGs include *Final Fantasy* and *Grand Theft Auto.*

Massively multiplayer online role-playing games (MMORPGs) are role-playing games that can be played via the Internet by many people at one time; an example is *World of Warcraft.*

Simulations

A wide range of simulations are available to provide players with the experience of actually doing an activity that they might not otherwise have the ability to do, such as driving a vehicle (e.g., flight simulators and car-racing games), raising a pet (*Tamagotchi, Nintendogs*), or urban planning (*SimCity*). Simulations are commonly used to teach science concepts that are difficult to otherwise explain. For example, simulations allow the exploration of gravitational forces on various planets and demonstrate how gravity impacts the speed at which objects travel through the air.

Tower Defense

A tower defense game challenges the player to protect a location (the "tower") from enemies. The enemies generally move on a grid or a predefined path. *Plants vs Zombies* is a tower defense game where the player defends his home from zombie invasion by using a series of plants with special powers.

Resource Management

In resource management games, the player has a limited supply of money or other items and is charged with doling them out appropriately to win the game. *Plants vs Zombies* is a resource management game as well as a tower defense game. Each item the player uses to defeat zombies requires currency to purchase the items, but the currency is limited in supply. The *Civilization* and *Rollercoaster Tycoon* franchises are also resource management games.

Music and Rhythm

This category includes games that require the player to re-create rhythms and/or music, such as *Rock Band, Guitar Hero*, and *Dance Dance Revolution*. Some are stationary games that do not require the user to move, while others, like *Dance Dance Revolution*, are considered exergames because of the physicality involved.

Sports

Games in the sports genre emulate sports played in real life; examples include *Tiger Woods PGA Tour* and EA Sports' *Madden* football franchise. Some sports games also include resource management mechanics to operate a sports franchise, including *MLB Front Office Manager*.

Additional Genres Specific to Kids

In addition to all the game genres enjoyed by kids and adults, a number of game types exist almost exclusively in the children's space, including a style of play based on sticker books and e-books. Many of these activities are not even games in the traditional sense of the word, particularly when the interaction is more open ended rather than goal oriented.

Sticker books are largely digital implementations of the traditional sticker book. The child can pick backgrounds and characters and add decorative elements to the pictures. The variations are numerous and range from simple dress-up activities to full-blown animation tools. In *Nick Jr. Draw & Play* the player can mix and match characters from lots of shows and watch them animate. In *Toontastic*, the player can drag and drop elements to make animated stories.

Figure 1.1 *Nick Jr. Draw & Play* allows kids to create scenes using backgrounds, animated characters, and coloring tools.

Nick Jr. Draw & Play HD image used with permission of Nick Jr.

E-books are digital representations of physical books. Some are simply digital versions of the book, while others are elaborately embellished with animations, narration, and embedded games. Design guidelines for e-books are discussed in Section Three.

Game Distribution Platforms

Games can be distributed in myriad ways depending on the platform the game will be played on. Distribution options also evolve at a rapid rate. As you begin to narrow down your technology and platform of choice, carefully examine the options available for distribution by searching online and asking colleagues.

Console games include Nintendo Wii and Wii U, Microsoft Xbox and Xbox One, and Sony Playstation. Players generally use a controller to play the game (though physically active interfaces like Kinect for Xbox are increasing in popularity). Games for consoles are either downloaded or come on a disk and have high-quality graphics, advanced gameplay, and networked gameplay with people around the world. These games often have massive budgets and take years to produce.

Increasingly, games are also available for download to consoles. In some cases, once the player owns a game, he can download additional content for the game via an online interface. PC and Mac owners can also still purchase CD-ROM games or download games from entertainment distribution marketplaces like Steam.

Handheld games, such as the Nintendo DS, are essentially console game devices that can be held in your hand. The content is still generally delivered on a cartridge of some sort that is sold through traditional retail channels. Handheld games are increasingly blurring the lines with mobile games, which are games delivered on smartphones, like the iPhone, or on tablets, like the iPad or the Google Nexus.

Mobile games, including those for smartphones and tablets, are delivered in downloadable files that are purchased in app stores (Apple App Store, Google Play, and Amazon are three well-known app marketplaces, and many more are in development). The apps for mobile devices range from small casual games, such as *Doodle Jump*, to games that require a significant investment of time and money to play.

Web games are played via an Internet browser, still most commonly on desktop or laptop computers. The technology development environment might be Flash, HTML5, or any number of other plug-in options, including Unity, which can also be used for developing games for other technology platforms. PBS KIDS, Nick Jr., and Disney all have large Web gaming sites for kids.

CHAPTER 2
What Is Game Design?

When I tell people I'm a game designer, the conversation generally goes something like this.

Me: I'm a game designer.
You: Oh, the programming?
Me: No, but I work with the programmers.
You: The art?
Me: No, but I work with the artists.
You: Ummm . . .
Me: I design the system, the rules of how to play. And then I work with the rest of the team, artists, programmers, writers, and so on to make the game playable. Sometimes if the game is really large, we have a producer who oversees and manages all the logistics. Then I get to focus on how the game works.

If you're a good game designer, most people won't notice your work. (They notice it only when you do a bad job.) It's sometimes hard to spell out exactly what a game designer does.

This chapter expands on various facets of game design, including game mechanics and how game design differs from other forms of media development.

How Do You Design a Game?

I like to think about game design as system design. I define the space in which the player will interact and detail every rule for interacting with the space. If the player can make an action that has not been accounted for in the rules, the system breaks. In digital products, that means a bug that could crash the entire system.

So game design is really about designing rules and thinking through all of the possible ways a user might interact with those rules or even how a user might break the rules.

Let's start with the children's game of tag.

Rules for Tag
- A single person is designated as "it."
- Run away from the it person.
- If the it person touches you, you become the new it.

As a player, you can mess with the rules of the game in lots of ways. For example, you might hide in the bushes or go inside. So a new rule might be established to create out-of-bounds areas.

Or you might want to make the game more interesting by blindfolding the it person. Freeze Tag is a great modification, where a player has to hold still when tagged by the it person. The person can't move again until another player touches her.

This is game design. What are the rules, and how can you modify them to make the game more interesting?

Once you start to become comfortable with the basics of game design, some people enjoy learning about the various frameworks and schools of thought on how to design a game. Designing games is an art, after all, so just as in television or other artistic practices, there are a lot of ways that you might approach the subject. Additional resources for game design tools are in the appendix. The next chapter also discusses what information goes into game design documents.

Game Mechanics

Game mechanics are another way of talking about the rules of a game. This is in contrast to the gameplay, which describes the actual experience of playing the game. Together, detailing the game mechanics and gameplay will provide a good picture of your game.

Common game mechanics include:
- Taking turns: In checkers, one person takes a turn. Then the other person takes a turn.
- Capture: In checkers, jumping over a checker of the other color allows the person to capture (or eliminate) the checker from the board. Capture the Flag is another game that uses this mechanic.
- Movement: In a board game, the player moves a token along a sub-divided path.
- Dice: The player has to roll a die to get a randomized number. This number could determine any number of things, including how far to move on a board.
- Match-3: The player has to match three particular items together in order to proceed.
- Goal: Most games have a goal or a mechanic that defines how the game ends, such as discarding all cards from your hand.

Game mechanics can be combined to create a wide range of gameplay experiences. How the mechanics and rules are communicated to the team to become a game is detailed in chapter 4, on documentation. If you want a heady and academic answer to the difference between game rules and game mechanics, see Google Raph Koster's blog "Rules versus mechanics."

How Game Development Differs from Other Media Development

Even experienced media developers are often caught off guard when they first encounter game design. These are some of the surprises I hear mentioned most often.

Iterative Development

When a person familiar with media production moves into games, the iterative nature of game design can catch them off guard. Small playable parts of the game are developed and tested with users, generally with placeholder audio and art. Then adjustments are made on the basis of the findings, which can sometimes lead to major changes in the original product vision. As these parts of the game are perfected, the various art assets and audio assets can be finalized.

If the game design and prototyping process is thought of as a television script, it's sometimes easier to understand. A writer doesn't get the script right on the first pass. It takes multiple rounds of review and revision to get to a place where everyone is happy continuing production. Games, unfortunately, cannot simply be revised on paper. They must be prototyped and adjusted until they have the desired feel, and then they can be polished and completed.

To Document or Not

The other way iterative development can cause heartburn is when the team emphasizes prototypes over documentation. Many of my projects start off heavily documented, and by the time we reach alpha, we're no longer updating documentation.

Prototyping is fast. We can make quick changes and see the impact. Updating documents takes time. We always maintain a voiceover list and asset list, but we're less likely to update design documents that detail mechanics.

If you have a particular need for the documentation to be updated throughout the process (e.g., for a client or for copyright reasons), make sure everyone on the team understands and that time is built into the schedule for everyone to adequately fulfill this responsibility.

File Sizes Are Not Limitless

Where television producers have to pay attention to the length of a segment or episode, developers have to be aware of file sizes, particularly for mobile games or games that have to fit on a disk or cartridge. It's not the fact that games are sometimes limited in size that catches people off guard but rather how the limitations manifest for production.

Audio files are space hogs. So we often end up concatenating files, where parts of sentences are recorded separately. Then the software plays the files we need. For example, "You found the red shoe!" could be divided into two files, "You found" + "the red shoe!" Then we can reuse "You found" in other sentences.

If may seem like a little thing, but when you're creating a literacy game and have hundreds of vocabulary words, every bit of saved space matters.

Accounting for User Interaction

Once the game is in the user's hands, you no longer have complete control of the experience. The user does. The user decides what button to push or where to move. Yes, you can guide the user, but the user has arrived at your game with an expectation of control. The user also decides when to leave!

This is perhaps the most difficult leap for producers moving into games. While creating the content, you have to account for all the different things the user might do with your game and decide how the game will respond.

Frequent and early user testing helps a lot (as discussed in chapter 15). No matter how hard you try to account for everything, the user will always find something you didn't expect.

CHAPTER 3
Game Design Documents

Game design documents take many forms and vary greatly in formality. I've designed games simply on a series of sticky notes as well as created hundreds of pages of detailed documentation. The goal, however, is to communicate the game experience to your team and stakeholders in enough detail so that they can build the game. This chapter explores common types of game design documents and the information that is generally included in them.

This chapter discusses game design documentation, including the types of design documents commonly used by teams, and provides a sample game design document.

Design Documents

Depending on the team structure, size, and preferences, a number of game design documents may be used during the creation process. In this section we describe common documents, though every team is different and uses different documents. The larger the game, the more documentation and the more formal the process. The names of the documents as well as the actual structure will vary, too. There is no one right model of documentation.

The documents to be discussed here include vision, technical design, production, quality assurance, and game design documents.

Because the discussion around the game design document occupies the majority of this chapter, the other design- and production-related documents are discussed first, even though some are completed after the game design document. Then the breakdown of the game design document follows.

Vision Document

The vision document is often the first formal document created and details the overarching creative goals and requirements. This document might include:

- Brief summary of the game (in two sentences or less)
- Educational goals
- Platform(s)
- Target audience
- Budget
- A handful of storyboards to define visual style and/or gameplay
- Timeline (including major milestones and release date)
- Team structure
- Market analysis (brief and optional)

Technical Design Document

Many projects will also have a technical design document (TDD), which the engineering team creates from the game design document. (Sometimes it's simply included in the game design document.) It details the major technical requirements, such as development environment, artificial intelligence, and code specifications required for production of the game.

Some find it surprising that even once a game is designed, the programming team generally still has to create another document that translates the design into technical-speak. Think of the game design document as the orchestral score and the technical design document as the sheet music for the musicians. Any musician could read the full score if she really wanted to, but it's cumbersome and not very efficient. The sheet music is tailored to what she needs to know and do. As game designers, we compose the score and the technical team uses that to write the different parts.

Production Documents

A variety of additional production documents may be needed for the game. These include documents to track art assets, voiceover scripts, and localization documents, which are used when the game is being shipped in a variety of languages.

Quality Assurance Documents

Quality assurance is an often underestimated part of production. Done properly, the QA team systematically checks that the game functions under all possible scenarios. The easiest way to make sure that the game is checked thoroughly is to create a QA testing plan, which documents every scenario that needs to be tested.

The testing plan is then divided among the members of the QA testing team, who begin playing the game repeatedly to make sure the game is bug-free. If they find a problem, the QA tester logs the bug (often in a bug-tracking database or spreadsheet), so that it can be checked by the development team. The log should detail what should happen (the expected outcome), what actually happened, and precise instructions for replicating the bug.

Game Design Document

The game design document (GDD) contains all of the details of the game, which usually includes:
- Platform, audience, genre, and other defining details
- Characters and environments
- Storyboards, which detail how the player will interact with the game
- User interface designs, including for menus, gameplay, and all supporting screens
- Gameplay and game mechanics
- Sound and visual effects (SFX and VFX) and when they're triggered

The sole purpose of the GDD is to explain how the entire game system will work. It shares the overall vision and then breaks it down into a framework that can be implemented. While the game designer and/or producer will largely "own" the GDD, most of the team will contribute to the document in one way or another.

A significant risk in creating a detailed GDD is that the team could become too bogged down in writing out the game rather than focusing on building, prototyping, and iterating on the game design. A good producer will be able to keep the team in balance with the right amount of documentation to keep everyone on the same page.

A number of sample GDDs are published online. Some documents are very technical and wordy, while others are storyboard driven, with large images and enough text to explain what happens behind the scenes. As an example of a game design document that I often use, the next pages are a document my team created for what ultimately became Kids' CBC *Little Wally Ball-y Ball* on iPad. It's a companion game for the *Monster Math* television show.

For this example, the *Little Wally Ball-y Ball* GDD contains the following parts:
- Version history: Every team handles this differently, but this section is a simple log of when the document has been updated. It's particularly helpful when you have a large number of people working on the document.
- Game Summary: A short summary of the game.
- Platforms: A list of what platforms the game will be developed for.
- Curriculum: If the game is educational, this section covers the curricular goals for the game. The level of detail depends on the team.
- Characters and Active Elements: This section details all the visual assets that are needed for the game, such as characters or objects that characters will interact with. Many objects will have multiple states, and those should be listed as well. For example, if a character stands still as well as jumps, both options should be listed.
- Game Layout: An overview of the user interface and relevant screens for the game. This should include wireframes where possible.
- Controls: How the user interacts with the game. It should list every button/tap and control.

- Voiceover: This is an overview of the needed characters and any other relevant notes on game audio. A number of games include variables where words can be interchanged. (e.g., "That's the number . . . five!" where "five" can be replaced by any number.) A separate document is used to outline the actual voiceover script.
- Game Flow and Elements: This is the longest and most intricate section, as it details all of the logic of the game. Essentially every interaction the player may take must be detailed.
- Puzzle Design and Levels: If the game has levels or puzzle design, this section will detail how those levels work, including how the player advances between levels.

As you'll see, the images in this document are quick mock-ups to simply demonstrate the interactions. We didn't need elaborate images to illustrate how to play the game. The goal of the document was to clearly outline how the game is played in such a way that the programming team could accurately implement the game.

Changes were made after the game went to production, including the addition of a tutorial on the first level. The Web version of the game was dropped, and the iPhone version was added.

Figure 3.1 A level from the final version of Kids' CBC *Little Wally Ball-y Ball* for iPad. *Little Wally Ball-y Ball* image used with the permission of Kids' CBC.

Little Wally Ball-y Ball: Game Design Document

Version History

7/25/12: Created
8/10/12: v2 finalized for review
8/17/12: v3 finalized for review

Game Summary

Little Wally Ball-y Ball is a game focused on slope. The goal of the game is to roll Wally Ball-y down Goo, who is dragged into shape by the player, to land on a target. The player manipulates the shape of Goo's body, and then Wally Ball-y rolls down Goo's body. By watching Wally take the path that the child has created toward the target, the user will gain a greater understanding of slope through various irregular geometric shapes, using visualizations and trial and error.

See *Contre Jour* iOS app for a sample reference.

Platform(s)

- Web
- iPad

Curriculum

Slope

Monster Math episode inspiration for content and curriculum
- 119: "Little Wally Ball-y Monster"

Characters and Active Elements

- **Goo**—Goo hosts the game and supports the player as needed. Goo is on the bottom left of the screen.
  - Goo's body has two parts:
    - Stationary body
      - His face (stationary body) animates with VO to address the player.
    - Malleable body
      - His outer edge (malleable body) animates in response to player input.
- **Wally Ball-y**—Wally Ball-y appears on-screen throughout the game. He initially appears in a predetermined place on Goo and then rolls up into a ball. He animates to roll according to the shape into which the player has manipulated Goo.
  - Behaviors
    - Once the game begins, Wally is perpetually in motion, rolling from the left side of the screen to the right.

- **Objects**—The following objects appear between Goo and the target.
  - o Springboard [Behavior: when Wally rolls over it, he is launched into the air]
  - o Ramp [Behavior: when Wally rolls over it, he rolls uphill]
  - o Rope [Behavior: when Wally rolls over it, it picks him up and swings him like a pendulum]
  - o Bubble (on Goo) [Behavior: when Wally rolls over it, Goo hiccups and launches him into the air]
- **Target**—A bull's-eye target appears on screen in the target location. It is either stationary or moves per level design.
- **Stars**—Stars appear on-screen that can be collected by the player during game play. They are stationary and disappear when collected.

Game Layout

- Single-Screen Game—No scrolling
- Background: Area background per level
  - o Level 1 (Easy): Monster Day Care Center
  - o Level 2 (Medium): Monster Playground
  - o Level 3 (Difficult): Monstrovia Town Square
- Game Area:
  - o Goo
  - o Wall-y Bally (on Goo)
  - o Objects (if applicable)
  - o Target
  - o Stars (3)
- Refresh Button
- Pause Button

Controls

- Web
  - o **Hear what a button says**—MOUSE OVER a button.
  - o **Manipulate Goo**—DRAG the cursor over Goo.
- iPad
  - o **Manipulate Goo**—DRAG finder.

Voiceover

- All lines are interruptible, unless noted otherwise in the Game Design logic.
- Goo is the voiceover character needed in this game. Wally Ball-y emotes only.
- SFX as designed below:
  - o On selection of buttons: Mouse click SFX (for Web), Tap SFX (for iPad)
  - o Whee SFX: Wally Ball-y emote for when Wally Ball-y rolls
  - o Star SFX: Sound for when player collects star
  - o Whoops SFX: Sound for when Wally Ball-y goes off-screen
- Voiceover listed in all caps, such as TRY_AGAIN or NUMBER_FINAL, are variables. See the game voiceover script for full list of variables.

Game Flow and Events

Game Flow Summary
1. Game Initialization
   a. Title screens and loading progress bar
2. Main Menu
   a. Button link to three levels of gameplay
   b. Button link to caregiver's information
3. Puzzle Selection Menu [Easy, Medium, Hard]
   a. Button links for all puzzles in that level
      i. Star icons for the number of stars collected in the puzzle
   b. Button link to return to Main Menu
4. Game Play Loop
   a. Present the puzzle
   b. Wait for player input
   c. Missed target response
   d. Correct answer response
5. Game Payoff
   a. Return to puzzle selection menus

GAME INITIALIZATION

- On start of the game:
  o Display title screens/logos
  o Simultaneously display Loading Bar
- Once assets are loaded OR title screens are displayed for five seconds (even if assets are already loaded), go to MAIN MENU
  o Please make the time requirement a variable that can be changed

MAIN MENU

- On-screen elements
  o "Little Wally Ball-y Ball" game name icon

Figure 3.2 A simple mock-up of the puzzle selection menu.

- Goo: Animated with VO (as indicated below)
- Wally Ball-y: Animated with VO (as indicated below)
- Caregivers [Button]
  - PC:
    - On rollover: VO: Goo: "Caregivers"
    - On select: Go to CAREGIVERS
  - iPad
    - On select:
      - VO: Goo: "Caregivers"
      - Go to CAREGIVERS
- Easy [Button]
  - Always unlocked
  - PC:
    - On rollover: VO: Goo: "Easy puzzles!"
    - On select: Go to Easy PUZZLE MENU
  - iPad
    - On select:
      - VO: Goo: "Easy puzzles!"
      - Go to Easy PUZZLE MENU
- Medium [Button]
  - Always unlocked
  - PC:
    - On rollover: VO: Goo: "Medium puzzles!"
    - On select: Go to Medium PUZZLE MENU
  - iPad
    - On select:
      - VO: Goo: "Medium puzzles!"
      - Go to Medium PUZZLE MENU
- Hard [Button]
  - Always unlocked
  - PC:
    - On rollover: VO: Goo: "Hard puzzles!"
    - On select: Go to Hard PUZZLE MENU
  - iPad
    - On select:
      - VO: Goo: "Hard puzzles!"
      - Go to Hard PUZZLE MENU
- On load of this page:
  - Line 1: VO: Goo: "Little Wall-y Ball-y Ball!"
  - Line 2: VO: Goo: "Pick a level!"
  - Line 3: "Easy!"
    - Simultaneously highlight Easy area.
  - Line 4: "Medium!"
    - Simultaneously highlight Medium area.
  - Line 5: "Hard!"
    - Simultaneously highlight Hard area.

- Wait for player input:
  - Timeouts (if no player input)
    - Play one of the following every 10 seconds, up to 60 seconds.
    - Timeout 1: VO: Goo: "Pick a level!"
    - Timeout 2
      - Web: VO: Goo: "Click the level you want to play!"
      - iPad: VO: Goo: "Tap on the level you want to play!"
    - Timeout 3: VO: Goo: "Choose a level to play!"
      - Simultaneously highlight level buttons.
- On selection of a button A:
  - Go to relevant area, as described above.

PUZZLE SELECTION MENU

Figure 3.3 A simple mock-up of the puzzle selection menu.

- On-screen elements
  - "Little Wally Ball-y Ball" game name icon
  - Difficulty Level Icon [Easy, Medium, Hard]
  - Puzzle Icons [1 to 10, pending level design] [Buttons]
    - One icon for each of the puzzles in that level
    - PC:
      - On rollover: VO: Goo: PUZZLE_NUM.
        - e.g., "One!"
      - On select: Go to GAME PLAY LOOP for the PUZZLE_NUM.

- iPad
  - On select:
    - VO: Goo: PUZZLE_NUM
      - e.g., "One!"
    - Go to GAME PLAY LOOP for the PUZZLE_NUM.
  - Stars
    - Each puzzle icon has three stars.
    - Stars are filled in to reflect the number of stars gathered in previous plays of the puzzle.
    - States
      - If collected: Filled in
      - If not collected: Gray with black outline
  - Back [Button]
    - PC:
      - On rollover: VO: Goo: "Back!"
      - On select: Go to MAIN MENU.
    - iPad
      - On select:
        - VO: Goo: "Back!"
        - Go to MAIN MENU.
- On load of this page:
  - Line 1:
    - If Easy Puzzles: VO: Goo: "Easy puzzles!"
    - If Medium Puzzles: VO: Goo: "Medium puzzles!"
    - If Hard Puzzles: VO: Goo: "Hard puzzles!"
  - Line 2: VO: Goo: "Pick a puzzle!"
- Wait for player input:
  - Timeouts (if no player input)
    - Play one of the following every 10 seconds, up to 60 seconds.
    - Timeout 1: VO: Goo: "Choose a puzzle to play!"
    - Timeout 2 (for Web): VO: Goo: "Click a puzzle to play it!"
    - Timeout 2 (for iPad): VO: Goo: "Tap on a puzzle to play it!"
    - Timeout 3: VO: Goo: "Pick a puzzle!"
      - Simultaneously highlight Level 1.
- On selection of a button:
  - Go to GAME PLAY LOOP for selected PUZZLE_NUM.

GAME PLAY LOOP

- On-screen elements
  - "Little Wally Ball-y Ball" game name icon
  - Goo:
    - Stationary body
      - Animated with VO (as indicated below)
    - Malleable body
      - PC: Click and hold to drag Goo's edges.
      - iPad: Touch and hold to drag Goo's edges.
  - Wally Ball-y

- ■ Perpetually in motion, if he can move (Goo's body or other objects may be blocking forward motion).
- ○ Target
- ○ Stars [1, 2, 3]
- ○ Refresh [Button]
  - ■ Refreshes the puzzle to the original state
- ○ Back [Button]
  - ■ PC:
    - • On rollover: VO: Goo: "Back!"
    - • On select: Go to PUZZLE SELECTION MENU.
  - ■ iPad
    - • On select:
      - • VO: Goo: "Back!"
      - • Go to PUZZLE SELECTION MENU.
- ○ Level objects, if designed for the puzzle
- ● Introduce puzzle
  - ○ Line 1: VO: Goo: "Get Wally Ball-y to the target!"
  - ○ Line 2 (for Web): VO: Goo: "Click and drag on me to change my shape and make a ramp for Wally Ball-y!"
    - ■ Simultaneously highlight the edge of Goo's body.
  - ○ Line 2 (for iPad): VO: Goo: "Use your finger to change my shape and make a ramp for Wally Ball-y!"
    - ■ Simultaneously highlight the edge of Goo's body.
  - ○ Line 3 (if new object in level):
    - ■ If Ramp: VO: Goo: "When Wally rolls over this ramp, he'll roll up it!"
      - • Simultaneously highlight object.
    - ■ If Springboard: VO: Goo: "When Wally hits this springboard, he'll rocket into the air!"
      - • Simultaneously highlight object.
    - ■ If Rope: VO: Goo: "When Wally hits this rope, it will pick him up and swing him!"
      - • Simultaneously highlight object.
    - ■ If Bubble: VO: Goo: "When Wally hits this bubble, I will hiccup and send him flying!"
      - • Simultaneously highlight object.
  - ○ Wally Ball-y rolls up into a ball.
  - ○ Go to wait for player input.
- ● Wait for player input:
  - ○ If Wally can roll, go to Wally Rolls.
  - ○ Timeouts (if no player input)
    - ■ Play one of the following every 10 seconds, up to 60 seconds.
    - ■ Timeout 1: VO: Goo: "Get Wally Ball-y to the target!"
    - ■ Timeout 2 (for Web): VO: Goo: "Click and drag on me to change my shape and make a ramp for Wally Ball-y!"
      - • Simultaneously highlight the edge of Goo's body.
    - ■ Timeout 2 (for iPad): VO: Goo: "Use your finger to change my shape and make a ramp for Wally Ball-y!"
      - • Simultaneously highlight the edge of Goo's body.

- Timeout 3: VO: Goo: "Change my shape to get Wally Ball-y to the target!"
  - Simultaneously highlight the edge of Goo's body.
- Player moves Goo
  - If player moves Goo, the edges of his shape drags accordingly.
- Wally rolls
  - Wally Ball-y Whee SFX.
  - If Wally rolls over a star:
    - Star SFX
    - Simultaneously star sparkles then disappears
  - If Wally rolls into a game object, Wally interacts as indicated in GAME OBJECT section.
  - If Wally rolls over the target, go to Puzzle Payoff.
  - If Wally rolls off-screen (otherwise missing the target):
    - Whoops SFX
    - Reset Wally to original position (rolled up). Reset Objects to original position (if relevant). Do not reset Goo's shape.
    - If third or subsequent time Wally rolls off-screen:
      - VO: Goo: "I'm not the right shape! Make me into the shape that will help Wally Ball-y reach the target!"
      - Display ghosted outline of a correct solution.
      - VO: Goo: TRY_AGAIN.
- Puzzle payoff
  - Wally celebration animation
  - Goo celebration animation
  - Line 1: VO: Goo: CELEB_FINAL
  - Line 2: VO: Goo: STARS_COLLECTED
    - E.g., "You collected three stars!
    - Simultaneously, stars appear on-screen.
  - Line 3: VO: Goo: COLOR_LINE
  - Go to PUZZLE SELECTION MENU.

CAREGIVERS

- On-screen elements
  - "Little Wally Ball-y Ball" game name icon
  - Little Wally Ball-y Ball is an interactive game experience to encourage your child to better understand geometry concepts. With exposure to different geometry challenges, your child will manipulate Goo to help Wally Ball-y accurately hit the target. We hope you enjoy playing!
  - Funded by (logo, logo, etc.).

Puzzle Design and Levels

- Content leveling
  - There is no in-game automatic leveling. Levels are created by puzzle type.
- Progress is saved between sessions (by cookie).
- Puzzles are landscape, no scrolling.

- Game objects
  - Game objects are items in the game that help Wally reach the target. Objects include the following:
    - Springboard [Behavior: when Wally rolls over it, he is launched into the air]
    - Ramp [Behavior: when Wally rolls over it, he rolls uphill]
    - Rope [Behavior: when Wally rolls over it, it picks him up and swings him like a pendulum]
    - Bubble (on Goo) [Behavior: when Wally rolls over it, Goo hiccups and launches him into the air]

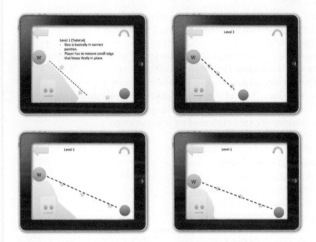

Figures 3.4–3.7 Mock-ups of example game puzzles.

Little Wally Ball-y Ball images and game design document used with the permission of Kids' CBC.

CHAPTER 4
Production

Each time you make a game, the production cycle will be a little different. While many things remain the same, each development team will have methodologies and milestones that it prefers. This chapter details the roles and development phases for an average children's game.

This chapter discusses development team members, such as producer, game designer, artist, programmer, user-tester, audio engineer, QA game tester, and advisers, as well as production milestones.

Development Team

When making a game, the team may be as small as one person who handles programming, art, and game design. But it's much more common for small teams of four or five people to create games, especially for mobile and Web-based games. Larger games, such as console games or virtual worlds, can have enormous teams of hundreds of people. But those big-budget games rarely happen in the children's market, so we'll focus on the roles for smaller-scale games.

Depending on the size and complexity of the game, some roles may have multiple people as well, such as several artists or programmers. Or several roles may be filled by a single person. For example, I've often served as producer and game designer. In all cases, game design production tends to involve a lot of interdisciplinary work, where team members are constantly working together.

Producer

The producer is the team leader and project manager, who is responsible for everything from budget, timelines, and resource management. The producer is also in charge of documentation and ensures that information moves appropriately through the team. On larger teams, there may be a hierarchy of producers (potentially including executive, senior, associate, and assistant producers).

Producers are particularly helpful at identifying and heading off feature creep—those questions that begin with "What if"—what if we add awesome feature X? What if our underwater hero has this amazing scene where he can fly?

The questions always come from a good place. The team is excited about the direction of the game and is genuinely trying to improve it. But scope changes and feature additions can not only add significant budget and development time to the project but also introduce risks to the codebase that cause more bugs. While it's never fun to be the person who has to manage these conversations, a good producer recognizes feature creep and has a plan for guiding the team through the discussion of whether the new feature improves the game to such a level that it's worth the time, money, and risk to add it.

Game Designer

The game designer is the person (or persons) who determines the game mechanics, rules, and gameplay that the player will experience. Some games also have level designers, who are game designers who specialize in creating the individual worlds of a game. For example, in the classic *Super Mario Bros.* games, a level designer created each of the worlds, including the iconic 1–1 through to the levels where the player has to navigate clouds, pits, and lava. The game designer creates a game design document, possibly in tandem with the art team that illustrates it.

The game designer might also serve as the writer for the game, or additional writers may be hired to create the story, voiceover, and other story elements.

Artist

The artist or art team is responsible for the visual aesthetic of the game, including backgrounds, characters, and user interface. On larger games, members of the team may specialize in particular areas, such as environment or characters. As with other roles, a hierarchy can exist in larger teams (e.g., creative director, senior artist, assistant artist).

Programmer

The programmer (or engineer, depending on the team's preference) is responsible for the code. Programmers take all of the pieces from the other teams and turn them into a working game. Programmers often specialize in particular types of code (referred to as languages) as well as tools. The hierarchy for programmers may include a technical director as well as engineers/programmers with varying ranks of seniority. Their skills are different from those of the IT team of a traditional company, though if you ask nicely, they will often help out! The programming team often uses the game design document to create a technical design document. While the game design document can generally be read and understood by most people, the technical design document is highly specific.

User Testing Team

The user testing team (or usability group) specializes in collecting player feedback, through either automated data or in-person observations and interviews. (User testing is discussed in chapter 15.) Small teams rarely have a dedicated testing person. They may instead use a freelance person brought in at particular milestones to review and test the game.

Audio Engineer

Every game needs (or should have) audio such as background music, sound effects, and voiceover. The audio engineer determines where and what sound is needed (often in conjunction with the game designer). For music and sound effects, the audio engineer will either compose them or oversee the composer. For voiceover, the audio engineer will oversee the recording session. (A voice talent director may also be part of that process.) Once all of the audio is prepared, the audio engineer will work with the programming team to implement the audio.

QA Game Tester

QA (or quality assurance) is the responsibility of at least one person, but often a team of people is tasked with making sure the game functions flawlessly, meaning no bugs that break the game or cause it to stop functioning and crash. The QA Lead will work with the development team to define a series of test cases so that the QA team can systematically play the game and confirm that everything is working properly.

Advisers

Not every team will have one or more advisers, but they are increasingly common in children's game projects. Advisers are stakeholders who give feedback to the team at regular intervals. Feedback may focus on creative direction or educational content. The more educational a title, that is, the more it focuses on a specific skill set, the more likely it is that the team will have a curriculum adviser to help ensure that the game is actually teaching the skill.

Production Schedules

Timelines for developing a game depend on complexity, team size, and number of partners involved in approvals. Console games and virtual worlds tend to have the longest schedules, with some games taking multiple years to produce. Mobile and Web-based games generally have much shorter development cycles, ranging from a few weeks to a year.

On average, children's games take from three to nine months to develop.

Production Milestones

The typical production schedule has a series of milestones or phases. Phases are largely defined by the state of the game, moving from discovery (where the game is largely unknown) to beta (where the game is being polished for release).

Discovery

The discovery milestone is the earliest stage and includes brainstorming as well as decisions related to platform, target age group, competitive analysis, budgeting, and other tasks related to setting the stage for development.

All of these decisions and criteria should be documented, often in a game vision document.

Preproduction

As the basic creative and business decisions are made, the preproduction period begins. (There is frequently a relatively seamless transition from discovery to preproduction, depending on the size of the team and the project.)

Preproduction includes staffing, team organization, technical tests, initial asset creation, prototypes of gameplay, and a lot of documentation, specifically the game design document. Many foundational decisions, such as those related to art style, will be made during this time.

Some larger games use this period to create a "Vertical Slice" or "First Playable" of the game, which is a working demo of the game. The vertical slice idea is borrowed from the sciences. It's a cross-section of the game that represents the major functionality the player will experience. It can be used as a milestone to greenlight the rest of the project, as well.

Production

Once the game moves into production, the game moves through a series of milestones or deliverables. These are often simply numbered milestones, such as Prototype 1, Prototype 2, and so on, that are assigned dates. With each milestone, additional features and functionality are added to the game so that it begins to take shape.

The prototypes generally include placeholder assets and scratch audio, rather than final assets, so the team has the flexibility to adjust the game interface and gameplay on the basis of feedback from user testing.

Alpha

While still part of the production cycle, alpha is a major milestone—the game is considered feature complete but is missing final assets. The game is often unstable and buggy at alpha. Some developers perform their first set of user testing sessions at alpha milestone. If major problems are found, having waited this long to find them creates the risk of costly changes, so I recommend testing earlier, even if informally. QA testing (quality assurance) also begins during the alpha period. A game may have multiple alpha deliverables; that is, a new build of the game is delivered weekly to show increasing progress and asset integration.

Beta

Beta is the final major production milestone. The game is feature complete and contains all final assets (e.g., art, voiceover, sound effects). QA testing is the primary focus of this milestone to ensure that the game is completely stable. The engineering team may also continue to streamline the code so that the game runs optimally. User testing often continues during this milestone so that the developers can fine tune the difficulty of the game (referred to as balancing).

If the game is being shipped in multiple languages, the game must also be localized to the other languages. While preparation for localization happens during earlier milestones (such as by recording the voiceover script in multiple languages), the integration of the localized assets generally begins during beta, once the game is considered stable and nearly final.

Online games and services sometimes have a beta period where the service is available to a private group. By this point in the development cycle, the game is largely stable and has passed internal QA tests. By making the game publicly available, even to a small group of people, the developers are able to further test the game and seed it with content and players.

Gold Master Candidate or Release Candidate

The final production milestone is the gold master candidate, or GMC, which means that the game is ready to be shipped. If the gold master candidate is approved as the shippable code, then it is the Gold Master, or final copy of the game. Some companies refer to this milestone as the Release Candidate.

Postlaunch Updates

Digital distribution through websites, app stores, and online marketplaces means that many games can be updated, even after the game is in the hands of the audience. Games that are updated after the fact still go through development milestones before being released to the public. Updates add new features, fix bugs, and balance (make changes to) the difficulty of the existing game levels.

CHAPTER 5
Finding a Developer

It's not unusual for someone to have an idea about a game for kids and not know how to program. Finding a developer who can execute your vision takes time. Any time you're hiring someone to do work that is in an area unfamiliar to you, finding someone you trust is paramount. It shouldn't feel like going to the mechanic and fearing that he'll tell you to do $600 in work on the brakes when you were just having the windshield wipers changed.

This chapter provides guidance for finding a developer, including:
- Sources for finding potential developers
- Requests for proposals (RFPs)
- Work-for-hire versus revenue share for developers
- Whether team members should learn to code

Where to Find Developers

Should you find yourself in the position of looking for a developer, try looking for options in these ways.

- Ask around. You probably know people who have made an app. Whom did they like? How did they find them? Use Facebook and other social media, too, as well as asking in conversation.
- Look at the apps that you loved from your research and find out who made them. Then call the developer.
- Go to conferences or local events to find local talent. Many local coding events are superfriendly to newcomers, and attendees are happy to talk about the industry.
- Ask around at universities to see if you might find student talent.
- Use online sites for locating freelance talent, but carefully review recommendations and talk to applicants several times before making a decision. The best rule of thumb is to remember that if it seems too good to be true, it probably is.

Once you have a shortlist of developers, start talking to their references. If you can find relevant people, also talk to people who worked with the developer but who were not provided as an official reference to get additional insight on how they operate. Talking to the developer is likewise going to be very enlightening as you talk about process and their approach to development.

While you're talking to references, also start getting to know the developer. If you're worried about protecting your idea, you can ask if the developer is willing to sign a nondisclosure agreement. (Not all will, but you can at least ask.)

As you talk to the developer, these are some topics to consider:

- Ask who will be your main contact throughout the process. Who is on the team, and what are members' backgrounds and experience?
- Find out about the team's development process. How does it handle bugs and testing? Are you expected to do it? Or do the members test in a systematic way?
- How do members handle change requests? Do you have some room for an iterative process or a period of discovery to refine the design?

- What projects have they worked on that are similar in nature?
- What tools or code do they have that will make the design and production process more streamlined?

If you're uneasy about your ability to understand tech lingo, pay attention to the way developers talk to you. Do they help you understand the lingo or dismiss you?

Then trust your gut. You are going to be paying the developer a lot of money, so you have to be comfortable.

Requests for Proposals (RFPs)

Some companies prefer to issue a request for proposals (RFP) to developers to solicit bids for a particular project. The RFP usually includes basic information about what has already been decided on the project, estimates of budget, and a launch date. Some RFPs detail the entire idea, and the company is simply looking for a developer to execute an idea. Other RFPs are more open, where a basic theme or guidelines are provided.

It's best practice to talk to the developers before sending them the RFP. This will ensure that the developers have time for your project and that they are open to the particular kind of project you're working on. You might also use this as an opportunity to verify that the general timeline you've applied to the RFP makes sense. I've seen a lot of RFPs issued in April for a product that has to launch by the beginning the school year. It rarely works out well.

Once you send the RFP, give the developers ample time to respond. Hold a conference call where everyone can ask questions. The common practice is to provide the same information to everyone who's responding.

When you make a decision, notify the other developers whom you did not select, if only to protect your future opportunities to work with them.

One other warning for RFPs. A number of IP owners issue RFPs before they're actually ready to greenlight the project. Whether it's intentional or not, the RFP process becomes a fishing expedition, where they are looking for interesting ideas. Experienced developers will sniff out these RFPs and drop out. Even if they stay in and respond, this practice can hurt your reputation with the developers. A good way to head this off is to have a consultant or developer who is not going to respond to the RFP review it and advise you of questions in advance.

Work-for-Hire versus Revenue Share

Which brings me to the very touchy subject of how to compensate a developer. I generally advocate that you pay the developer on a milestone schedule in a work-for-hire agreement. Not surprisingly, the idea people are not happy when I say this.

I understand that money is tight, especially for startups or those who are moonlighting. But this is an incredibly competitive business. Your idea is one in hundreds of thousands. Odds are against you. And developers know this. You're not the first person to ask for a partnership.

Should the revenue share arrangement be your only path to market, then approach compensation as honestly and respectfully as possible. Share your track record of success (if you can) or dazzle them with your knowledge of the market, your familiarity with the competition, and your plan for marketing and monetizing the app. And hang in there. It could be a long road to find the right partner.

Should You Learn to Code?

Inevitably, when I'm asked how to find a developer, the question that follows is "Or should I learn to code?" Is it important to learn how to program in order to design games or work in the games field?

In general, my answer is yes, learn to code, even if only a little. If a designer internalizes how programming works, this knowledge can transform design documents and improve communication with the coding team, making for a better production experience.

But programming is not for everyone, and not every project is the right moment to learn. If you have a lot riding on the game, it's not the right project to learn on. If you're trying to avoid the cost of a developer, it's not the right time to learn. (You'll likely end up paying someone to fix your mistakes!) But if you have time to work on a game in a low-stakes environment (perhaps even think of it as a hobby), then you will be happy to have tried the experience.

In case you didn't guess, I have learned how to program. I've tried a number of languages, including BASIC, HTML, Flash, and JavaScript. Flash was particularly helpful once I began to internalize object-oriented programming, which is a coding paradigm. It's noteworthy only if you're picking a language to learn, in which case I recommend something that lends itself to this. Or ask around among developer friends for what they recommend.

I rarely program anymore, however. It's often a frustrating experience since I don't have enough time to dedicate to it. It drives me mad that a single forgotten semicolon can turn my carefully crafted lines of code into a string of error messages. I much prefer to work with programmers who have learned to architect stable and reusable code. Yet knowing how programming works means I can have intelligent conversations with the programmers about the features and the restrictions of the code.

It also means I can write design documents in a way that assists the programmers in architecting the site. The engineering team will still need its own technical documents, but a savvy game designer can create a game design document in a way that assists this technical translation and streamline development.

So that's why I learned how to program and why I advocate that anyone with an interest and an appropriate project make the attempt. In the worst case, you'll have a lot more respect for those who bring your ideas to life!

CHAPTER 6
Game Business Models

The subject of how to monetize games for kids can be touchy. But the reality is that it's a business and a lucrative one for many. The same business models used in games in general can be used for children's games; however, some present challenges, depending on the age of the audience.

This chapter summarizes business models in the gaming industry and the challenges they present in the children's media sphere, including:
- Premium games
- Free games
- Ad support
- Free-to-play and in-app purchase games
- Monetization and ethical considerations for children's games

Premium Games

A premium game is a one-time purchase that gives the user access to the entire game without making another purchase. Premium games are especially common on the mobile app stores. Downloadable markets, such as Steam from Valve Corporation, also offer premium games.

Pricing Strategies for Premium Games

Determining the fee you should charge for premium games can be done in a number of ways. I tend to analyze the options from three angles.

Analyze the Competition

First, examine the apps that you think are most like yours in quality, brand recognition, and depth of content. What's the average price of those apps? This is a time to be very honest with yourself about who your competitors actually are. Are you really in competition with Nick Jr., or are you competing with smaller, independent brands that generally rank between 200 and 400?

Estimate Purchases

Estimating the number of purchases also requires that you be honest with yourself. I tend to estimate three numbers—failure, success, and hit. For example, if I'm developing a music creation app for iPad, I talk with fellow developers about the average performance of such games, scour websites that provide estimates or sales numbers for the target marketplace, and collect any and all information I can find in postmortems and other articles online. Once I've done that, I decide that anything less than 10,000 purchases is failure, success is 30,000 purchases, and a hit is more than 60,000 purchases. (Remember that these are made-up numbers.)

Some developers go so far as to assign probabilities to the various numbers, but I prefer to keep it simple and align the development budget with success number. So if I estimate 30,000 purchases at $0.99 (and the platform publisher takes 30 percent), my development budget must be under $20,790 if I am to plan conservatively to recover the costs.

Reverse Engineer the Price

It's also helpful to reverse engineer the costs starting from a budget estimate. The budget estimate must include all costs, development, updates, marketing, award submissions, legal fees, Web hosting, and so on.

If my app in the Apple App Store is going to cost $50,000 to develop and I predict 30,000 purchases, then I need to charge $2.99. Also be sure to include the revenue share for the marketplace you use (e.g., Apple takes 30 percent of sales in the App Store).

30,000 * $2.99 = $89,700

With Apple's cut, that's $62,790 in total sales. (Apple does not allow anything other than increments of .99, so that's why I ended up with a $2.99 price and $12,000 in profit. A price of $1.99 would come up almost $8,000 short in this situation.)

Setting the Price

Once I've done all these exercises, I generally find that I've reached a price and budget that I'm comfortable with. Or at least I can reasonably justify the decisions.

It also helps to look at all the options side by side. Table 6.1 shows the number of purchases needed to break even at various price points. Seeing these data often serves as a gut check for your pricing strategy. Is the number of purchases actually achievable?

The mobile markets are especially vulnerable to "race to zero" pricing strategies. It's a crowded market, and a lot of good content is available free or very inexpensively. Success in the marketplaces is often quantified by placement in the top charts. A lower price increases the probability of purchases, and more purchases translate into a higher rank on the top charts. A higher rank on the top charts equals more potential purchases.

Table 6.1 Number of purchases required at various price points in order to recover development costs of $25,000, $50,000, and $100,000

Store price	App Store (30%)	Development Budget		
		$25,000	$50,000	$100,000
$0.99	$0.30	29,000	72,200	144,400
$1.99	$0.60	14,400	36,000	107,700
$2.99	$0.90	9,600	23,900	47,800
$3.99	$1.20	7,200	18,000	35,900
$4.99	$1.50	5,800	14,400	28,700

This may make you feel that you should price your app as low as possible. However, prices are slowly increasing. It's not uncommon to see $2.99 games for iPad and to see those games perform well, especially from high-quality developers. If you've spent time building your brand, you should be able to command a higher price and forgo the Top 10 mindset.

It also helps to realize that higher price points generally result in more revenue. For example, here's the profit from 30,000 purchases at three different price points.

30,000 purchases * $0.99 = $29,700 * Apple's 30% = $20,790
30,000 purchases * $1.99 = $59,700 * Apple's 30% = $41,790
30,000 purchases * $2.99 = $89,700 * Apple's 30% = $62,790

If your metric for success is simply number of purchases, then, yes, a $0.99 strategy is likely to get you more purchases. Most people are far more comfortable shelling out one buck than three. But the lower price pays out in revenue only if you sell a significantly larger number of apps.

If your metric for success is revenue, then a $2.99 model can pay out well. (If you were selling the app for $0.99 but wanted to make the same profit that you would selling at $2.99, you'd have to sell about 90,000 copies instead of 30,000.) Sometimes it might make more sense to put less emphasis on making the top lists.

The great thing about the marketplaces is that no price is set in stone. It's obviously easier to go down in price than it is to raise the price, but you can list games at a lower price and include that it's on sale. Be sure to account for these sales in your overall revenue projections.

Free Games

The free model is considerably easier to explain. The game is free. The user never has to pay for it. (If the user encounters advertising or a paywall, those are different models that are described next.)

Why Release a Free Game?

Marketing, usually. Before the mobile markets, many Web games were released free of charge simply because they were a good avenue for marketing televisions shows and other brands.

Nowadays in mobile, it's not uncommon to see free games for the same reasons. If you can't monetize your game directly, release it free in the hope that it will drive traffic to your other products (or games).

Other games are free because they were funded by another source, such as grant funding.

Some free games are trial versions of premium games, created to allow the player to try out the game before making the purchase. Sometimes these have a link to the marketplace where you can buy the full version, and sometimes they include an in-app purchase or option that allows you to upgrade directly. So it's a little more than a simple free model, but it's not quite advertising supported, as is discussed next.

Advertising-Supported Games

Many free games are monetized via advertising, either as cross-promotion for in-house brands or for third parties.

As with all other forms of media, advertising can be dicey when children are the intended audience. It tends to have a poor reputation; advertisers are assumed to be greedy and bombarding kids with inappropriate images, so proceed with caution. However, cross-promoting in-house brands or even closely related partnerships is generally accepted, especially if done tastefully.

Advertising networks are services that deliver ads on your site/app/content. Website banner ads are the most ubiquitous, and mobile devices often use interstitial ads that appear in between levels of content. The ads are delivered automatically to your site after a bit of code (referred to as an SDK or software development kit) is installed into your codebase. They generally require an Internet connection to update the ads, though they usually have some content automatically built in to avoid blank screens.

Advertising networks are not uncommon on desktop websites, but they're less common in the mobile markets, due to privacy concerns and ethical considerations. A few ad networks can reliably filter ads to distribute selected companies or specialize specifically in child-friendly brands, but many systems are home-grown. If you consider working with an advertising network, be sure to comply with all legal requirements. Be on the safe side and get a professional with applicable experience to consult.

Additionally, if you're including any sort of advertising or cross-promotion within your game, clearly label the ads. Don't create hidden links that a child might accidentally tap on, especially if it would take the child out of the current site or app to another website. Instead, open the links in a new page and/or use a confirmation message to make sure that the user really wants to go to another location. Finally, if at all possible, limit ads to the parent areas whenever possible, especially when creating content for very young users.

Free-to-Play Games or In-App Purchases

Candy Crush Saga is one of the most successful free-to-play games in recent history. To play the game, the player matches candies into groups of three, either horizontally or vertically. While the game can be played without spending money, the player is presented opportunities to purchase additional moves and features that will assist with gameplay. This model defines a free-to-play game—the player does not have to spend money to play the game.

Zynga is largely responsible for putting the free-to-play model on the map, notably with *Mafia Wars* and *Farmville*. The model has always been controversial, but the concerns focused around aggressive monetization strategies in general (not specifically about children) because the games were limited to Facebook. Now that the games are available on mobile devices, they're much easier for kids to access, elevating concerns that children are able to spend large amounts of money accidentally or without understanding the implications.

But in-app purchases are successfully used in children's games. Highlights for Children uses them in their *Highlights Hidden Pictures Puzzles* app. Sesame Workshop has them in *Elmo Calls*. Free-to-play games are commonly free to download and then cost money to purchase additional content. Sometimes it's called the freemium model—get the base app for free (or dirt cheap), then buy expansion packs and add-ons for cost within the app.

Organizing your content into a base package that can be expanded makes a lot of sense for many apps. For example, if Hidden Pictures didn't do expansion packs, you'd either end up with a giant app that costs a lot of money or 40 different apps on your computer. What if all your electronic books were individual books instead of bundled into the Kindle or iBooks app? This episodic approach to content makes organization easier on both the developer and the end user.

Figure 6.1 The *Highlights Hidden Pictures Puzzles* app features in-app purchases for additional puzzles. The bundles of puzzles are available in the Parents area of the app.

Highlights Hidden Pictures™ Puzzles image © Highlights for Children, Inc. used by permission.

Defining Characteristics of Free-to-Play Games

These are basic features that define free-to-play games.

The initial download or install is free. At the simplest level, free-to-play games are available to play without any advance purchase. You can then begin playing the game free of charge before you begin to encounter points where you are presented the option to pay money for additional content or features.

The game can be played end-to-end without ever paying. Free-to-play games often start as skill-based games, where you can quite manageably play without paying, but then transition into levels where it is possible to play for free but it would be far easier if you paid.

The game has barriers to slow players who do not want to pay. I spent $7 on *Candy Crush Saga* and have progressed through hundreds of levels. But that means it has taken me a lot longer than some people. I've been stuck on some levels for a week or more because I can play only in short spurts. *Candy Crush Saga* is designed so that you have five lives to use. If I use a life by not successfully completing a level, it takes 30 minutes to replace that life. I can have a maximum of only five lives. So if I use all five lives and put the game down for 2.5 hours, I'll then refill all five lives. But I can also pay $0.99 or I can post to Facebook that I need help (thus spreading the word) to be able to play more sooner.

In this way, while it's possible to play the game without paying, it will take you far longer to progress through the game. In other words, you will pay with your time.

The game does not offer an option to unlock all content for a single high sum of money. Some games offer an option to download all the content for some large amount of money, like $50. That's more inline with in-app purchase models for content than it is with the idea of free-to-play games.

Analytics are used to identify pain points and target users who are most likely to pay. Data can be used for good and also to make money. Which brings me to the psychology of free-to-play.

The Psychology behind the Monetization of Free-to-Play Games

A few years ago, Roger Dickey (of *Mafia Wars* and Zynga) coined the phrase "fun pain." It's the parts of the game that involve grind. Grind tends to be an annoying experience or task that you tolerate because you know it gets you to the fun parts.

In free-to-play models, the game will progress to a point where you encounter a pain point and then offer the player a way to release the pain, generally by paying for an item.

In *Candy Crush Saga*, the puzzles have a limited number of moves you can make. If you don't win the board in that number of moves, you lose a life and have to start over. I'm often one or two moves from winning the level when I run out of moves. I can then pay $0.99 to get more moves (and win the level! FUN!) rather than start the board all over again (PAIN!).

Another way the practices of free-to-play games are labeled, which is far more disconcerting, is to call them coercive monetization. The player is essentially manipulated into making a spending decision under emotional duress or with limited knowledge. The example I've given is one such example, but other practices include:

- Limited time offers for bundled content, making it appear to be a better deal.
- Levels of abstraction, especially with virtual currencies. Think of when you travel to a country with a new currency, such as going from the United States to a European country. You have to keep in mind the value of the new currency (the euro) relative to your home currency (the dollar) when making purchases. There's clear value assigned to those currencies, making the translation fairly simple math. But in-game currencies are abstracted, and their dollar value is not always clear.
- Discounted currency (e.g., buy 100 coins for $2.99, 200 coins for $3.99, and 500 coins for $4.99). It's just like buying raffle tickets—1 for $2 or 3 for $5! So, on top of the problem of valuing a virtual currency, you now also have to account for bulk discounts.

- Requiring payment to maintain your current level of status or collection. You've played the game and unlocked 100 levels and content, but you'll lose all that progress unless you pay to "store" your progress. What if Facebook suddenly said you need to pay us to keep all your friends, photos, and status updates? You're emotionally attached to the content.

If you haven't played any of these games, I'd highly suggest you spend some time playing to experience firsthand the monetization points and the emotion you feel when presented a purchase option. It's powerful stuff even for us as adults.

Which is why it's incredibly challenging to think about whether it's possible to use the model with children.

The State of the Debate on Whether Free-to-Play Games Should Be Used in the Children's Market

In the business of children's app development (and in children's media in general), we generally have two bottom lines—financial and social good.

In other words, we need to make money. But we also need to do what's best for the children.

That means the business models available to our products generally comprise subscriptions, premium (one-time payments), free (under the logic that it's marketing for another product), advertising supported, and free-to-play either as in-app purchases for content/episodes or through the model discussed earlier. In an era where audiences increasingly want free options, the performance of free-to-play games like *Candy Crush Saga* makes it a compelling model to explore further.

It was not so long ago that in-app purchases for content and episodes were condemned in the children's community. Best practices around in-app purchases have emerged, including the use of gesture gates that slow children from making accidental purchases. High-profile apps, including those by established brands (e.g., Sesame Workshop, Highlights for Children) and new brands (e.g., Kidaptive), use in-app purchases for content with little pushback. One year from now, will we be talking best practices in free-to-play games rather than arguing about the model?

But is it actually possible to ethically implement free-to-play for children?

The answer is not easy. Simply the idea of free-to-play for children is fraught with a lot of heated discussion. If a developer were to attempt the free-to-play model as designed in *Candy Crush Saga* but aim for the kid audience, the backlash would be enormous. Kids simply don't have the psychological maturity to be able to evaluate whether the purchase decisions are actually good or coercive. Most adults struggle with that, too! So any developer attempting a free-to-play model would have to make significant modifications to the model.

Without those aggressive monetization strategies, it would almost certainly mean a significant reduction in profit. It's not unlike subscription models—the number of people willing to regularly pay for a subscription service is fairly small compared to the number of people who will use a free trial option. In a free-to-play game, the gates to slow down kids from making poor decisions would also slow down revenue. Parents would have to be involved to manage how much money a child can spend, and as soon as you add another layer the profits drop. Given that some companies are using this model successfully, it certainly is an option for developers, though they have to understand the risks and rewards.

CHAPTER 7
Competitive Analysis and Identifying Market Opportunities

There are hundreds of thousands of games and education apps in the Apple App Store alone. That covers Apple devices only, not Android or any other mobile app market. It's a crowded, competitive space.

That means there's a very high probability that someone has already made the product you're thinking about or something very, very, very similar to it. And it would be very sad to waste any of your hard-earned dollars on something someone else has already made.

This chapter aims to provide insight to the children's games market, with information on how to perform a competitive analysis and use that to identify potential opportunities.

Competitive Analysis

If you already have a project in mind, the competitive analysis and vision document will likely happen simultaneously.

If you are looking for an idea or if you are still sorting out details like target audience, platform, or even the content, use the competitive analysis as an opportunity to identify opportunities in the market. Then repeat the competitive analysis once you narrow the details.

But, in such a crowded space, how do you conduct an exhaustive search?

- Talk to people. Ask for recommendations of things that are like the product you're considering. You don't have to give away your secret sauce, but ask around with as much detail as you can to get recommendations of products that might be comparable.
- Search everywhere with as many possible keywords as you can think of. Not only will you uncover your competition, but you'll also gain valuable intel on how to structure your own keywords (assuming you make it all the way to launch, that is).
  o Keep a log of your keywords.
  o Don't limit yourself to just your target platform. Check all platforms that you can reasonably afford. If something is on Android but not iOS, it's not that hard to port.
  o Look up apps in the stores, like Google Play or App Store, and follow similar or recommended apps to see what else you find.
  o Search app intelligence services, like App Annie and Distimo, and app review sites, like 148 Apps or Apps Playground.

If you don't have an idea in mind but are instead looking for opportunities or gaps in the market, try these things.

- Follow RSS feeds for new apps. You can use a reader to see all of the apps that are released to the App Store. It's thoroughly enlightening to see everything coming out on a daily basis. You'll see trends. You'll see bad ideas and good. And you'll start to see opportunities.
- Play as much as you can, and not just things that are in your target demo. Inspiration can come from anywhere. And the more you play with a savvy eye, the better you'll understand the market.

- Review categories in the App Stores. Apple, for example, regularly creates categories for various subjects. It's pretty easy to explore these and identify where there's a wealth of content and where there's opportunity.
- Read industry reports (resources for this are listed in the appendix). They are often a gold mine for trends and opportunities in the market.
- Do exhaustive keyword searches on various keywords, especially educational curriculum concepts. As mentioned earlier, keep track of these for future use, but also study what has zillions of results and what appears to be lacking. (Use your brain on whether it's actually needed—if a term turns up few or no results, this might also mean that there's no market for the app!)

This is not a short process, and it should frankly continue throughout the entire development process. You never know when a competitor might pop into the market ahead of you.

PART 2

Understanding Kids

Image used under Creative Commons Attribution License by Flickr member Jen Robinson.

This section provides an overview of childhood, including what kids are able to do at various ages. For the purposes of this book, we are primarily concerned with children under 12, so the sections are divided into babies and toddlers (0–2 years), preschoolers (3–5 years), early elementary-school kids (6–8 years), and tweens (9–12 years). A brief discussion of teens is also included as well to provide a full picture of childhood.

The section ends with two chapters that are not necessarily about kids themselves—one is on societal considerations when developing games for kids, and the other is about user testing, which will be quite helpful when you need to get additional (or more specific) information from kids.

CHAPTER 8
Child Development Overview

We were all kids once, so why does a game designer need to bother knowing about child development? Familiarity with child development provides guidelines for what kids can do at various ages, which in turn allows us to design for the particular needs of our audience. As adults, we are far removed from the hallmark experiences of childhood.

For example, as you read this, your brain is automatically processing the words. While you may encounter an unfamiliar word from time to time, which will slow you down, you are not actively engaged in figuring out what every single word says. The process of reading is automated so you can focus on meaning, not how the individual letters come together to make a word. As adults, we don't remember what it's like to have to sound out words and put the meaning of a sentence together bit by bit.

We also do not really remember what it's like to not have the motor skills necessary to perform a simple task accurately. One of my favorite studies demonstrating differences in kids' and adults' motor skills is a research study from 2003, performed by Juan Pablo Hourcade for his dissertation research. He created a computer task requiring subjects to use a computer mouse to click on two buttons that were separated by a few inches. He tracked the paths of the subjects between the time of clicking on the two buttons.

The paths of adults were very efficient, because they have refined motor skills. The paths of five-year olds are dramatically different—the paths meander all over the page before reaching the target. The paths of four-year-olds are even more dramatically different, showing their developing fine motor skills.

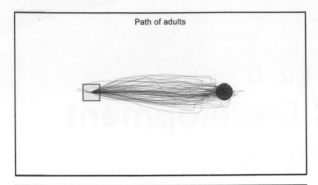

Path of adults

Figure 8.1

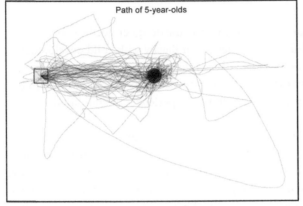

Path of 5-year-olds

Figure 8.2

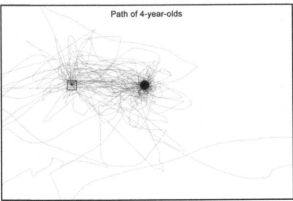

Path of 4-year-olds

Figure 8.3

Figures 8.1 to 8.3 show the results of a study where people were asked to use a computer mouse to click on two targets. The lines show the paths of the mouse. Adults **(Figure 8.1)** were the most efficient. Children who were five years old **(Figure 8.2)** and four years old **(Figure 8.3)** were quite inefficient. This shows their developing motor skills and lack of accuracy.

Images used with the permission of *Juan Pablo Hourcade*.

This study remains one of the simplest ways to demonstrate the difference in motor skills—or the ability to coordinate body movement—at various ages. While it was performed with a computer mouse, the idea remains the same, no matter the technology. Adults have better motor skills than the average five-year-old. And the average five-year-old has better motor skills than the average four-year-old.

Developmental psychology researchers regularly devise tasks like these to highlight the particular skills and the differences among children.

So, while kids will eventually become adults with advanced skills and abilities, they go through a number of stages on their way to becoming fully developed adults. These stages include unique cognitive and physical challenges that game developers must understand in order to make truly engaging games for children. The best way to understand their needs is to understand child development and to test products with the target audience throughout the production cycle.

The remainder of this chapter provides a general landscape of child development, including:
- Piaget's experiments
- Educational philosophies
- Caveats for applying developmental psychology guidelines

Piaget's Experiments

Whenever child developmental psychology is discussed, Jean Piaget is bound to be mentioned before long. He was the psychologist largely responsible for defining the field of child developmental psychology in the 1900s. Among his notable work was the identification of a number of cognitive stages, starting from infancy, that outline the changes in thinking skills as the child progresses from concrete, literal thinking to the logical and abstract thinking of an adult.

To illustrate the various stages, he created tasks that children perform differently depending on their current cognitive stage. These Piaget tasks remain one of the most powerful ways to demonstrate the differences between young children and adults.

For example, ask a young child (perhaps a three-year-old) which is more—a whole banana or a banana cut into pieces? The child will likely tell you the banana cut into pieces is more than the whole banana. The child has yet to master the idea of conservation—the idea that certain properties remain the same even when an object undergoes a physical transformation. In this case, even though the banana was cut into pieces, it's still the same amount of banana. By the time the child is seven or so, she will have mastered this logical thinking skill.

Perhaps the best-known Piaget conservation task involves glasses of water. When a young child is shown two identical glasses of water with the same amount of water (as shown in Figure 8.4), she will tell you that they are the same. Then ask the child to pour one glass of water into a significantly differently shaped glass, such as a tall, skinny glass (as shown in Figure 8.5). Then put the glasses next to each other (Figure 8.6) and again ask which glass has more. The child will now say that the taller glass has more, even though moments ago she correctly observed that the two glasses had the same amount of water.

YouTube is full of people demonstrating these tasks. I highly recommend watching these videos or, even better, trying them out on children in your life. (You should know that some parents get really freaked out by the results, even though it's totally normal for a child to make these errors. Parents think their children should understand these things. So perhaps be prepared with resources that explain the phenomenon, just in case.)

Figures 8.4–8.6 Image of Piaget water glasses test
One of the best-known Piaget tasks testing children's cognitive abilities is the water conservation task, in which kids are tested on whether they recognize that the amount of water is the same, even when the glasses are shaped differently.

Images used with permission of the author.

While Piaget tasks are great for demonstrating the cognitive differences between kids and adults, it is important to note that his work is not the only way of framing childhood. In fact, much of his work has been challenged in recent years. It should not be the sole measure of a child's ability.

Educational Philosophies

Beyond the various stages of development, the field of child development has a number of educational theories, which guide how children learn and acquire information. One of the most popular is constructivism, or the idea that knowledge is developed (or constructed) through experiences. Constructivists emphasize discovery and hands-on exploration as well as problem-based learning in education. Games are largely constructivist in nature, especially sandbox games, like *Minecraft*, where the user can construct his own world.

Another theorist, Lev Vygotsky, developed the zone of proximal development. It defines what a person can do alone and what she can do with help (scaffolding). While the concept was originally focused on social interactions, the zone of proximal development is relevant to game design, especially educational game design, as game designers are constantly tasked with how to help the player become more experienced and master new tasks.

All told, there is no one correct approach to games and educational psychology (though many people will happily debate whether one theory is more important than another)! It is really a matter of personal choice and what connects best with your own beliefs. Most designers, including myself, use a blended approach that is loosely organized around constructivism but also borrows from all of the best practices, research, and theories. In the end, the goal is to create games that motivate, support, and encourage the child to learn the desired content and have a generally positive experience while doing so.

To return to the original question of why developmental psychology matters—without developmental knowledge like that provided by these studies, a game designer is working in a vacuum. If you make what you think will be interesting and usable for the child, you are likely to be very wrong. You can't simply rely on your gut.

Developmental Psychology Offers Guidelines, Not Absolutes

The next few chapters are guidelines depicting normal development for four childhood age ranges, including babies and toddlers, preschoolers, early elementary, and tweens. While teens are not a focus of this book, they are briefly discussed to provide a full picture of childhood. Early childhood is marked by rapid changes in children's lives, so there's no perfect way to divide the age groups. For our purposes, the chapters are divided by industry trends (e.g., the children's entertainment industry often targets programming for children ages 3–5 separately from programming for kids ages 6–8).

Each chapter begins with a brief summary that defines the age group, followed by the major milestones that define the group for cognitive, verbal, mathematical, social/emotional, gross motor, and fine motor skills. It's followed by challenges particular to the age group that somehow don't fit in the milestones. Finally, each chapter ends with example games for that age group.

But remember that the chapters are guidelines. Developmental psychology is not a science of absolutes. For each milestone, there are wide ranges that are perfectly normal.

I may say that at age 4, a child should be able to grasp the concept of numbers up to five. But there are always children who master it earlier and those who master it later. It does not necessarily mean that there is something wrong. There is a wide range of "normal" abilities.

A child's development is influenced by myriad factors—gender, birth order, parenting style, environment, education, culture, and so on. Because of this, some children master skills earlier than others and some take longer. Studies find all sorts of variation based on factors like these, including variation in the ages children in European cities begin walking as well as research that indicates that children in Zambia reach motor milestones earlier than American children. It also matters whether a child is taught or encouraged to practice a skill—20 percent of nine-year-old children do not develop kicking or throwing skills because of a lack of practice.

Every child develops in his own unique way. All children follow a generally similar pattern and meet widely held expectations, but the details are always different for each child.

For developers, this means designing with a wide range of abilities in mind. One child who uses your product may be experiencing the technology for the first time. Another child might have dozens of hours already logged on the device. Frequent user testing with a variety of ages and abilities will help you understand the range of abilities of your audience as well as the impact of any cultural or environmental differences.

CHAPTER 9
Babies and Toddlers (Ages 0–2)

Babies and toddlers are learning the basics—how to walk, talk, and interact with the world. Games for babies and toddlers should support their innate love of exploration and encourage caregiver-child interactions.

This chapter discusses the developmental milestones of children up to age 2, including:

- An overview of their cognitive development
- Learning styles
- Language and communication skills
- Mathematical thinking
- Social and emotional development
- Motor skill development
- Abilities related to music and creative arts
- Developmentally appropriate games for this age

Figure 9.1 Image used with the permission of the author.

Developmental Milestones

Technology use and gameplay are going to be very limited for very young children, mostly because they're cognitively and physically not able to complete most tasks. They are figuring out the basics—reaching, grasping, crawling, sitting up, acquiring basic language, and so on—and that makes it difficult for them to play anything but the simplest games.

As babies and toddlers master basic movements, they also gain the ability to explore. Touching, tasting, shaking, dropping, and moving objects provide a large amount of sensory information about the world around them. They develop the pincer grip, or the ability to hold an object between the thumb and forefinger, providing even more information about texture, shape, and density.

Experimenting by exploring everything around them is the most common way babies and toddlers gather information. They try lots of things, including learning through sensory exploration by picking up and tasting objects. They will play with just about anything, be it mud, clay, paper, water, paint, or bubble wrap.

They are also beginning to learn about cause and effect. When a child discovers that a basic task like pushing a button can cause another action, she will be delighted and repeat it over, and over, and over, and over. She also will repeatedly attempt tasks until she reaches mastery. While it looks dull to adults, this is a key play pattern for children. They're practicing simple problem solving and will happily show you what they can do. "Look what I can do!" or "Watch this!" are phrases very commonly uttered by toddlers.

Language and Communication

Young children use pointing (gesturing) to communicate before talking. The gestures and grunting eventually give way to words.

Around 12 months of age, a child understands approximately 50 words and speaks a handful of words. She generally acquires one new word a day. By 18 months, the number of words understood grows to 200 words, with 68 or more spoken words. She'll acquire two or more new words a day. She will also comprehend simple sentences and phrases, such as "Stop that" or "Are you hungry?"

By 24 months, children can learn one to two words a day, understand at least 600 words, and average 200 spoken words. When speaking, however, they often need a familiar adult to translate, as their pronunciation is hard to understand. Around this time, a toddler begins to infer the meaning of words from the context.

Literacy

Although babies don't read, they are developing the earliest skills related to literacy. Babies and toddlers enjoy sounds, including those in nursery rhymes and songs. When books are repeatedly read to them, they may begin to identify objects. By age 2, children will also retell favorite parts of books and rhymes or sing along with songs.

Early play with language, including playing with the sounds of words (phonics), is a key foundation of literacy.

Mathematical Thinking

While children at this age don't show much understanding of numbers, they begin to show an understanding of small quantities of one or two by age 2. They begin to interact with simple puzzles and shape identification around this time as well. They also begin to explore spatial skills by filling and emptying containers.

Toddlers also begin mastering basic patterns, such as ABAB. If you present a two-year-old with a puzzle picturing *banana apple banana apple banana*, she will learn to tell you that the *apple* is the next item in the pattern. Related to patterns, toddlers will also recognize patterns in daily activities, such as bedtime routines.

One of the most significant accomplishments for babies and toddlers is object permanence, or the idea that an object continues to exist even when it cannot be seen, which is also an aspect of mathematical and spatial thinking. As babies, they believe that if something is not visible, it no longer exists. But around 18 months they begin to understand that an object that is hidden under a blanket still exists, even though it cannot be seen. It's one of the reasons babies so love peekaboo. They think you disappeared!

Social and Emotional Development

In general, babies and toddlers prefer to be with familiar people. Babies are interested in looking at other babies, but they rarely play together, at least in the sense of what most adults expect.

Figure 9.2 Peekaboo is a fascinating game for babies who have not yet discovered object permanence.

Image used under Creative Commons Attribution License by Flickr member Toshimasa Ishibashi.

Toddlers engage in parallel play, where they engage in the same activity as another child in the same location, but the play is still solo. For example, two children might each build a block tower side by side. They would indicate that they are playing together, but their activities are individual.

This style of play slowly gives way to associative play in two- or three-year-olds, where they begin to interact. Tempers are likely to flare as this is the first time children are engaging in social negotiations.

In general babies and toddlers are just starting to experience emotions and struggle to control them. Tantrums begin, in part, when a child wishes to express frustration but does not have the vocabulary or cognitive ability to express how he's feeling.

Figure 9.3 When kids engage in parallel play, they are actively engaged in the same activity but not interacting with each other.

Image used under Creative Commons Attribution License by Flickr member Biofriendly.

Motor Skills

By 12 months of age, babies have coordination of thumb movements, enough to hold a cup or use a spoon or crayon, though with unreliable accuracy. If they attempt to color, children may take visual interest in the marks, but they will not recognize the marks as related to writing or drawing.

By 24 months, manual dexterity will have improved to a point that the child can generally turn a page of a book without tearing it or build a tower of about six blocks high.

Ninety percent of children will walk by holding onto furniture by 13 months. By 24 months, 90 percent of children are able to kick a ball forward, jump, run, and climb.

Music and Creative Arts

By age 2, toddlers take interest in nursery rhymes, stories, and other literacy activities. They are unlikely to recognize print in any meaningful way, but they are beginning to form the associations of print with the spoken word. Frequent reading activities help children develop vocabulary and knowledge of the world around them.

Music and rhythmical movement activities are also wildly popular with babies and toddlers. Toddlers begin to sing along with tunes. Their pitch may follow the general contour of the song (e.g., increasing pitch as the song goes up the scale), though they are rarely accurate. They are also unlikely to actually pronounce many of the words correctly. But they love to sing, which makes karaoke games like *Rock Band* a popular choice.

Example Games for Babies and Toddlers

Babies and toddlers are developing all of their skills, so the simplest interactions provide plenty of challenge. Arguably, many of the interactions for babies and toddlers barely qualify as games. But it's really all they need! The simplest games can reward the child for just moving the computer mouse or touching the keyboard.

Many of the technology devices have accelerometers and other tools for tracking movements like tilting or shaking. Big movements, like shaking their whole arm, are far easier for young children than the precise movements, like tapping a button.

The iOS app *Sago Mini Sound Box* allows players to tap the screen to create small balls. When the device is moved, either by tilting or shaking, the balls bounce around and make music. Additionally, the game is designed for button mashing, or pressing buttons rapidly and at random. This is normally frowned upon in gaming as it's akin to cheating. But for babies and toddlers, button mashing and random movement is the norm.

Babies love faces, and toddlers love identifying themselves and other familiar faces in photographs. The cameras in smartphones and tablets make it easy to create customizable content with photos of the family.

Cute as Can Bee allows a story to be customized with photographs. A parent or older sibling will be needed to set up the photos, so keep them in mind when developing the instructions and interface.

Figure 9.4 *Sago Mini Sound Box* is a simple interaction for young children. The player has only to tap on the screen to be rewarded with visual and audio feedback.

Sago Mini Sound Box image used with permission of Sago Sago.

Figure 9.5 *Cute as Can Bee* allows the content to be customized with faces of friends and family, which is well received by babies and toddlers.

Cute as Can Be image used with permission of Picture Me Press.

CHAPTER 10
Preschoolers (3–5 Years)

Preschoolers, or children ages 3–5, are explorers who get into everything and believe in magic. They take pleasure in mastering tasks and showing off their skills. They're egocentric and often sticky.

This chapter discusses the developmental milestones of children ages 3–5, including:
- An overview of their cognitive development
- Learning styles
- Egocentrism and perspective taking
- Executive function
- Language and communication skills
- Mathematical thinking
- Motor skill development
- Social and emotional development
- Abilities related to music and creative arts
- Developmentally appropriate games for this age

Figure 10.1 Image used with permission of Natasha Pilkauskas.

Developmental Milestones

Preschoolers have an innate curiosity and love of learning, which is a great opportunity for game designers. The preschool years are when many kids have their first significant experiences with digital media such as television and games.

Preschoolers spend all of their time learning, whether it's practicing fine motor skills or preliteracy skills of letter recognition and sounds. Every experience is educational to them, but all of this learning is in the form of play. It's not work. While older kids may say, "Ugh, math," preschoolers are eager to learn and show off what they learn.

Much of preschoolers' learning is driven by developing common-knowledge scripts for how to interact with their world. As adults, we've developed thousands of these scripts. For example, a common-knowledge script is how to eat at a restaurant—arrive at the restaurant, ask for a table, review the menu, order, eat your dinner, pay the check, and leave. We have also adapted these scripts with numerous variations—for eating at a buffet, at a wedding, at a fast-food restaurant, at a prix fixe restaurant, and so on. The script continues to expand as we experience more and more restaurants in our lives.

Preschoolers are forming the foundation of those scripts. They're learning how to eat at a restaurant and what steps are involved, and as that knowledge grows they expand and modify the scripts. The basics must be in place first.

They also learn through repetition. Like babies and toddlers, they are working toward mastery of the subject and will endlessly practice tasks. Then they will happily show you what they have learned to do!

Experimentation is also a critical part of their learning style. It takes many forms—stacking blocks in different ways, testing boundaries by seeing how far they can walk away from a parent before being called back or by making funny sounds over and over.

Physical humor resonates with preschoolers, particularly because their cognitive skills are not advanced enough to understand word-based humor. That said, they will experiment and take cues from your reactions. For example, if a child modifies a song to sing, "If you're happy and you know it, touch your chicken nugget," and you reward her with a giant laugh, she'll be encouraged to keep experimenting and playing with language.

Egocentrism and Perspective Taking

Preschoolers are very egocentric and struggle to understand another person's perspective. In a physical sense, they do not yet understand that what one person sees differs from what another person sees. For example, when a librarian is reading to a group of children, she sees all the children's faces, whereas the children see her and possibly the back of the other children's heads. Asking the child to draw what the librarian sees is the easiest way to test whether he is able to understand that people have different physical viewpoints. Preschoolers will draw their own viewpoint, not that of the librarian.

Another way to test their understanding is to stand in a room with a child and ask the child if you can see various objects. Once you are familiar with objects in the room, move to a location where you cannot see an object but the child can. Asking the child if you can see things that are within only the child's visual field will demonstrate whether he's able to take your perspective into account. Most likely, if he can see the object, he'll say that you can see it, even if you can't.

Beyond the physical manifestation of perspective, preschoolers also struggle to understand that a person may have different beliefs or goals. If the child likes yogurt, he will assume that everyone loves yogurt as well. Person-versus-person games are tough at this age for this reason. It's actually a really complex idea to understand that each player has a different goal. For example, in a game of checkers, one person's goal is to capture black pieces while the other person's goal is to capture the red ones.

Executive Function

Preschoolers are generally impulsive, acting quickly rather than thinking things through. The ability to control impulses as well as to plan for and make rational decisions requires a suite of skills referred to as executive function. It's an area ripe for game design, too, as many games are related to these skills.

One of the best-known developmental psychology experiments related to this is the marshmallow experiment, which also demonstrates a key challenge for preschoolers—self-regulation, or the ability to control impulses. In the marshmallow experiment, children are told that they can have one object now (often a marshmallow or other highly desirable object) or two if they wait a specified period of time. The researchers then leave the room and observe the child. Those who demonstrate delayed gratification and waited for the period of time in order to get the second treat have been shown to have better life outcomes in numerous scenarios, from SAT scores to body weight. What is also amazing is the strategies kids employ to help them wait, which include everything from petting and talking to the marshmallow to moving to a corner of the room.

Today, a number of researchers are looking at how to improve executive function in everyone from preschool age through adults. A number of childhood games are part of developing executive function. *Red Light Green Light* is a game of inhibition control, where children have to stop and freeze when someone says "red light" and move toward a goal when the person says "green light." Games of memory matching help children develop their working memory (the things that we store short-term in order to perform a task).

Language and Communication

In the preschool years, language and communication skills rapidly develop and conversation begins. Three-year-olds know the alphabet; four-year-olds can recognize letters and know that letters create the sounds in words; and five-year-olds are at the very beginning stages of reading and writing.

Vocabulary Development

During the preschool years, a child's vocabulary explodes. Three-year-olds have a vocabulary of 1,000 words or more and speak in approximately six-word sentences. The vocabulary of four-year-olds is around 2,500 words, and they learn between four and six new words a day. Five-year-olds have a vocabulary of 4,000 to 5,000 words.

For three-year olds, their vocabulary tends to grow by groups of words (or schemas), such as animals or fruits. As they age, their vocabulary still grows by categories, but the categories broaden in meaning. For example, shoes are not just "clothing" but also another category with lots of ideas within (flip flops, sneakers, rain boots, snow boots). By age 5, the child also gains new language based on areas of interest. If the child is interested in dinosaurs, he will learn numerous words related to dinosaurs, including the names of animals and related terminology (e.g., plant eaters, meat eaters).

Communication

When speaking, three-year-olds are improving in their pronunciation. (One can usually figure out what they are trying to say.) They are likely to confuse pronouns and mix up the past and irregular tenses ("He runned down the street" instead of "He ran down the street"). They are just learning how conversations work, and storytelling unfolds therein. During conversations, three-year-olds have a lot of trouble waiting their turn to speak and often want to interject. They ask a lot of questions, as they are trying to figure out how the world works.

Four-year-olds speak in complex sentences and know the rules for sentence structure. Even though they understand how conversation works, they still struggle to wait their turn during group conversations. Five-year-olds are very conversant and are able to wait their turn during group conversations. They speak clearly and can convey a story in full paragraph length. When they share a story, they include all the relevant details.

Three-year-olds like to tell stories about their lives but often leave out relevant details, and the listening adult must play detective. For example, a typical conversation could be like this:

Child: I saw a dinosaur today.
Parent: Where did you see a dinosaur?
Child: At the museum.
Parent: You went to the museum today?
Child: With grandma.

Older preschoolers still prefer to tell stories about themselves but are much better at filling in all the relevant details.

Three-year-olds can understand and follow simple directions (take off your shoes and hang up your coat). They understand explanations with concrete examples. For instance, "Wind makes a sail boat move across water. See what happens when you blow on your boat in the bathtub." Thanks to their large vocabulary, five-year-olds can follow multistep directions.

Reading and Writing

Three-year-olds will sing the alphabet and may recognize certain letters from words they commonly see in writing, such as the first letter of their name. Four-year-olds are learning to write letters and understand that letters go together to create the sounds of words. They often try to write (made-up) words, but these sometimes appear as gibberish.

At three, children begin to listen to and understand stories, and they become fully adept at it by age four. Their listening comprehension is very high. Most can remember the events of the story and can tell you about the characters in a given story. They pay particular attention to the sound of words and are great with rhymes. In fact, most four-year-olds can name four or so words that rhyme with a given word (like cat, bat, mat, hat, fat). By age 5, their comprehension has advanced to the point where they are now able to understand stories about concepts they have not personally witnessed. This also reflects their cognitive growth, improvements in not just literacy but also in conceptualization and imagination.

Mathematical Thinking

During the preschool years, children master many of the basics of mathematical thinking. They explore basic numeracy concepts, including counting and quantity. By age 3, they can count to five and often higher. They may also think they're counting higher but begin saying numbers seemingly at random ("ten, eleven, fifteen, fourteen, eleven"). They also start to recognize written numbers. By age 5, they're starting to understand the patterns that allow them to count in the teens and beyond. In other words, they can append "twenty" to count "twenty-one, twenty-two, twenty-three" and so on. They can also count backwards and start to be able to count by tens.

Three-year-olds can identify quantities up to about five items as well as begin using estimation words like "few" and "many." By age 5, they can identify or enumerate quantities to 10, estimate small numbers of objects, and begin to understand terms like "more than" and "less than."

During the preschool years, children begin performing informal addition and subtraction, especially if groups of things are put together, such as two apples and one banana to make three pieces of fruit. Counting on fingers and pointing to objects are key parts of performing these tasks, so much so that taking away their ability to point to objects significantly reduces preschoolers' accuracy in performing simple addition tasks. When designing games that involve counting, keep in mind that children will point at and touch the objects on screen.

Understanding of spatial relations and geometry expands rapidly during the preschool years. Children move from simple shape recognition into recognizing complex shapes and 3D figures. They also start solving simple puzzles where a piece is set into a shape (such as a square into a square shape) and then move to increasingly difficult jigsaw puzzles or other complex building materials.

Preschoolers also learn to take apart shapes and to construct different shapes, such as making a square with two triangles. Similarly, they learn to find objects and geometric shapes hidden within other shapes. It's a complex skill (and popular game mechanic) that continues to develop throughout childhood.

The vocabulary acquired by preschoolers includes numerous mathematical concepts beyond basic words related to quantity. Related to a preschooler's understanding of space is her ability to correctly use positional language, such as "up," "down," "above," and "between," which develops during these years. It's not uncommon for preschoolers to struggle with these labels.

It's also not uncommon for preschoolers to struggle with language related to the passage of time. Going back to their egocentrism, they tend to see time as being all now, now, now. Five minutes from now means little. But eventually, they begin to recognize patterns in the day as well as develop an understanding of increments of time (e.g., five minutes versus two hours, tomorrow versus a week from now, yesterday versus last month).

They also develop the vocabulary and abilities to compare, sort, and match objects on numerous dimensions. When sorting, many preschoolers struggle with the ability to switch between rules. A card-sorting task is an easy way to show the lack of flexibility.

In a card-sorting task, the child is first asked to sort objects on the basis of one dimension, such as color. Then the rules are changed and the child is asked to sort on a different dimension, such as shapes. For example, the child might be asked to put blue objects in one box and red in another. So all blue trucks and blue flowers go in one box. Then red trucks and red flowers go in another. When the rules are changed, the trucks go in one box, regardless of color, and the flowers in the other. Kids who are still developing the flexibility to shift between rules will struggle with the rule switch.

Another key math skill is the ability to recognize and complete patterns. While as toddlers children learned simple patterns, preschoolers continue to advance in their ability to recognize complex patterns of three items (e.g., ABCABC) or with multiple dimensions (e.g., red square, blue triangle, red triangle, red square, blue triangle, red triangle).

Motor Skills

Preschoolers continue to acquire motor skills, such as learning to throw a ball, as well as refining the skills they've already acquired.

Gross Motor Skills

If you've ever been around a preschooler, you know that they are incredibly physical and energetic. They're constantly running, jumping, and climbing.

My favorite descriptive phrase is that preschoolers are mastering postural control of gravitational forces. In other words, they're learning to walk in a straight line, including balancing to walk on a narrow line or balance beam. They're not very good at standing on one foot. And it's really difficult to get them to stand with their weight equally distributed. (Dig out a Nintendo Wii Balance Board and watch what happens.)

During the preschool years, kids transition to walking on stairs with alternating feet. When they first learn to walk on stairs, they'll always step up or down with the same foot, bring the other foot to the same step, and then step up or down with the lead foot.

In almost everything they do, they do it with too much gusto. In other words, throwing a ball is not a very efficient or accurate endeavor for preschoolers. But with practice they improve over time. With so much energy expended, they also tire quickly (not to mention that they have relatively short attention spans), so they need frequent breaks.

Preschoolers also don't stay where you put them, which is especially problematic when playing games on a device that requires the player maintain a certain distance from the television, like the Kinect. Kids tend to move toward the television when playing games while standing up. Even when staying in place, they tend to fidget, which can cause problems for those using motion-controlled game mechanics.

Fine Motor Skills

As mentioned in the introduction to the child development section, preschoolers are really inaccurate with their fine motor skills. The study by J. P. Hourcade showed how even four- and five-year-olds can vary wildly in ability.

During the preschool years, children spend a lot of time coloring, tracing, and refining their fine motor skills to learn to control a writing tool. They also learn to accurately control other tools like scissors and eating utensils. At the same time, their ability to accurately hit targets with a computer mouse or on a touchscreen ranges in accuracy and improves with time and practice.

Preschoolers are also notorious for switching hands and fingers unpredictably. For example, they may eat multiple meals with their right hand, only to suddenly switch to their left. (Hand preference really doesn't stabilize until elementary school.) Particularly when developing games for touchscreens, developers should remember that kids can use either hand at any time for interactions. At any time, they may be obscuring part of the screen and key information with their hand.

Social and Emotional Development

During the preschool years, children learn how to make friends and play with others. The ability to make friends is dependent upon concurrent emotional and social development.

Recognizing and Managing Emotions

Emotional development begins with the ability to label feelings and generally starts with the basics—happy, sad, scared, and mad. As children move through the preschool years, they are able to label more and more emotions and to separate their distinctions. Three-year-olds are just beginning to learn to manage their emotions, but may fall apart under stress. Four-year-olds generally manage their emotions well. Five-year-olds are able to control their emotions and comfort themselves under most circumstances.

As kids learn to label their own feelings, they also learn to identify the feelings of others. Eventually, this leads to understanding the reasons behind the feelings, such as feeling angry because a sibling took her toy.

As their emotional understanding grows, preschoolers begin to understand that they may have different wants and feelings than others, which is the ability to take in the perspective of others. A child demonstrates a complex level of understanding if she recognizes that she is angry that the teachers didn't bring out the trains for playtime while also realizing that her friend is happy because the blocks are available instead.

Sense of Self

Preschoolers begin to develop a sense of self and individual preferences. This comes out a lot in "look at me!" behaviors, where they want their trusted adults (parents, teachers) to watch them practice skills. As they progress through the preschool years, they become more and more aware of their abilities and begin to compare themselves to others. Self-esteem also begins to develop around the age of five.

Social Development

The development of children's social interactions is closely tied to their ability to recognize and moderate their emotions. Three-year-olds have friendships with other children. Friendships among four-year-olds are often based on a bond created by common interests. Four-year-olds start to play together without the assistance of an adult. They continue and expand upon the cooperative play. Five-year-olds are able to both form and maintain friendships. They easily enter groups already at play and create the play situation for themselves. They are eager to develop new friendships and see this as a means of gaining acceptance from the group.

Interactions between preschoolers evolve from parallel play as a toddler, where kids play side by side with similar toys, such as blocks, without interacting, to associative play, where they begin to interact around the same toys. Tempers are likely to flare between children as this is the foundation of cooperative play, where kids are learning how to play together.

Cooperative play emerges when kids are around three and continues all throughout childhood. Cooperative play is a key time for kids to practice social negotiations. Kids must learn to respect the playspace of others. In other words, knocking down another person's block tower is not cool. They also use cooperative play to practice negotiating, by asking for their wants and making compromises.

Adults generally moderate play sessions for preschoolers, particularly since conflicts inevitably arise. Three-year-olds are not able to resolve the situation on their own. An adult is needed to model acceptable behaviors. As they grow older, they also learn to establish roles and settle conflict. For example, if five-year-olds are playing a pretend game of school, they might be heard saying, "Let's play school! I'll be the teacher and you be a student!" They are aware of and responsive to their friend's feelings during play. If a conflict arises, they will try to settle it themselves before seeking adult help.

Pretend play, sometimes referred to as role playing or sociodramatic play, is an important part of developing and practicing social interactions that begins during the preschool years. The pretend scenarios give children an opportunity to explore a variety of social situations and emotions. Pretend play not only helps children to explore and learn social rules but also allows them to practice conflict resolution. This type of practice furthers a child's ability to have positive social interactions with peers.

Going back to learning styles for preschoolers, pretend play is also part of preschoolers' common-knowledge script development, which is why they frequently reenact scenarios of doctor, school, house, restaurant,

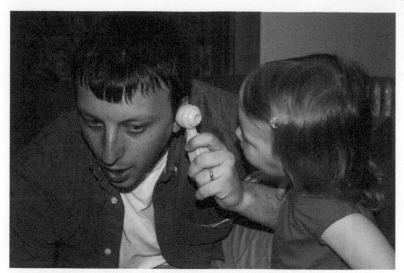

Figure 10.2 Preschoolers love sociodramatic play or role playing. It also provides an opportunity to explore social interactions and emotions.

Image used under Creative Commons Attribution License by Flickr member Abigail Batchelder.

or any number of common daily experiences. It also provides opportunities for practicing emotions and recognizing the emotions of others. For example, when playing doctor, the child will ask the patient how he is feeling and attempt to find a solution to make the patient feel better.

Music and Creative Arts

Music is both an enjoyable and an educational opportunity for preschoolers. At a practical level, singing, clapping, and playing simple instruments help them develop basic pitch-matching and rhythm skills. Dancing along to songs also helps them develop gross motor skills. *Dance Dance Revolution* and other dance games were not specifically designed for kids, but YouTube is full of videos of kids playing these games and having a great time.

Learning to sing a song by heart plays to preschoolers' desire to master topics. Songs also present simple ways to present information and vocabulary to kids, whether it is body parts or sciences. (Check out some of They Might Be Giants' or Barenaked Ladies' albums for kids.) Songs also support children's literacy development with rhymes and playing with sounds.

The development of preschoolers' fine motor skills is particularly evident in their artwork. They start by combining basic scribbles and shapes into representations of the things around them. One of the earliest artistic representations kids make is known as a "tadpole human," which is literally a circle with a single line. It looks like a tadpole, but the child will tell you it's a picture of a person. Four-year-olds also draw flowers, houses, animals, and other things that they see in their everyday lives.

Example Games for Preschoolers

When designing for preschoolers, it remains important to foster exploration and discovery through simple interactions. At this age, however, it's also possible to begin introducing longer and more complicated interactions and rules. Games for preschoolers should be simple enough that they can celebrate and show off when they master the skills but also grow with their quickly improving skills.

Because preschoolers are learning everything about the world, most content focuses on educational information, from letter names through to skills like categorization. For example, *Sid's Science Fair* is an activity that encourages preschoolers to practice categorizing objects on different dimensions, such as shape and color.

Whether you call it magic or naiveté, digital products for preschoolers can do things that older kids will sniff out as a scam. The iPad app *Sneak* uses the camera and microphone to detect motion and sound. The child has to sneak up on the device quietly in order to snap a picture of a monster.

Another favorite is *Monster Meter*. You use the app to scan the room for monsters. All it does is show you the camera view of the room and overlay a radar-like scanner of the room. Then it tells you how many monsters are in the room (and smartly includes an option to make sure the answer is always no monsters). It's beautifully simple concept and an excellent example of how to create content for the magical beliefs of preschoolers.

CHAPTER 11
Early Elementary Kids (Ages 6–8)

Kids ages 6–8 are beginning to discover their independence and preferences while expanding their social networks. They are increasingly able to strategize and to keep multiple goals in mind, leading to their ability to play more complex games.

This chapter discusses the developmental milestones of children ages 6–8, including:
- An overview of their cognitive development
- Learning styles
- Mastery of different perspectives
- Executive function
- Language and communication skills
- Mathematical thinking
- Motor skill development
- Social and emotional development
- Scientific thinking
- Developmentally appropriate games for this age

Figure 11.1 Image used with permission of Andra Abramson and Paula Ross.

Developmental Milestones

By ages 6–8, most children traditionally begin full-day formal schooling and learn to read, write, and answer formal math problems. Children's social networks expand rapidly with similarly aged peers during this time, largely in part because of attendance at school, which leads to great strides in social skills.

Between seven and nine years of age, there's a significant shift in media use habits. During the preschool years, many parents control children's media consumption habits, often quite strictly. But, as children mature and begin to express their own opinions and exercise control over their preferences, parents relax rules on media time. Because of this, the majority of children eight years of age and older play games at least occasionally.

As kids this age become immersed in formal schooling, they begin to engage in classroom-based learning techniques, which may include homework, memorization, and other classic school skills. At the same time, kids still also learn through play and exploration, making their learning styles varied.

With age also comes an increasing attention span, allowing kids to participate in longer play sessions. Where preschoolers struggled to switch rules for simple tasks, early elementary-age kids are capable of switching tasks. They're also able to hold multiple rules in mind. Because of this, they're able to enjoy more complex games. (Some would even argue that this is when kids really become able to play most classic game mechanics.)

These children are beginning to explore their ability to make choices of their own and are very curious to try new things. Give them choices when possible, while guiding and supporting them in finishing the task or project that they choose. When things do not go as planned, they can get quite frustrated. Scaffolding (or help in activities) is an important tool in games, especially educational games. Ways to implement scaffolding are discussed in chapter 19.

Mastering Different Perspectives

Remember that preschoolers struggle to understand different perspectives. For example, when a teacher is standing at the front of the room, the teacher sees the class, whereas each student has a particular view of the teacher. The idea that what I see is not the same as what you see is a tough concept.

Around age 6 or so, kids become better at understanding differing perspectives. They also become better at managing the abstract idea of differing goals—that my goal is potentially different from your goal.

The game of hide-and-seek is challenging for these reasons. The seeker has to find the hider. The hider has to find a place where the seeker can't see him, which means that the hider has to be able to:

1. Understand that the seeker can see things differently than the hider
2. Strategically pick a place where the seeker won't be able to see the hider when the seeker isn't even around
3. Remain in that place, quietly, until found

That's a lot of work and perspective taking!

Around this age, a lot of kids begin playing team sports, such as soccer and baseball. These are great perspective-taking activities as well as opportunities to practice social negotiations.

In soccer, for example, one team, say the Red team, is trying to get the ball into the Black team's goal. But, at the same time, the Red team must protect its own goal from the Black team. Both teams have opposing goals, and now the child must not only understand that we have differing goals but make plans and actions based on those two different goals.

Additionally, because kids are playing together as part of a team, they have numerous chances to interact socially. They have to follow the rules of the game. But they also begin to learn that when the entire group of players agrees, they can change the rules. For example, if they're short a few players in a neighborhood game, is it okay to play with fewer players on each side? What if someone has to leave early? How does the group decide to modify the game and rules? What if there is a disagreement on scoring? Team sports allow kids to interact to practice cooperation and negotiation in a structured setting.

Figure 11.2 Team sports, such as soccer, become popular for children ages 6 and up and are a developmentally appropriate activity to help them practice social skills as well as understand differing goals and perspectives.

Image used under Creative Commons Attribution License by Flickr member Chip Griffin.

Language and Communication

In the elementary years, kids continue to grow in their language and communication skills, but the main event is the development of their ability to read. Many kids will read some words as well as act out and retell stories before age six. During this time, however, they learn to decode and process words on paper. By age eight, they will even be writing their own stories to share.

Vocabulary Development

Kids continue to acquire language at an estimated rate of 20 words per day. As they learn to read, their sources for learning new words grows as well. They begin to acquire words that are related to things they may have never seen in person, such as information about plants or animals, or words related to abstract concepts.

Verbal Communication

By early elementary age, kids have learned to take turns while speaking, though they will still need reminders, particularly when they are excited. They sometimes confuse words, especially words with irregular forms, but they generally speak in complete sentences.

Comprehension

Kids ages 6–8 can follow multiple-step instructions, such as "Go to the closet, get the broom, and bring it to your dad in the garage." They also improve in their ability to retell stories. Rather than simply explaining the highlights of a story, they will retell the story in chronological order and include the major plot along with some subplot elements.

Their ability to understand words expands beyond physical description and into function. So a broom is no longer a yellow stick with a prickly brush; it's used for sweeping and cleaning.

Reading

Around age 6, children begin the transition to independent reading. It is a long process and will take many years before the child shows full fluency as a reader, but the early stages will emerge. Children develop confidence sounding out words (often referred to as decoding) and recognizing common words (often called sight words).

Playing with letters and letter sounds is a common exercise for kids of this age as it continues to support their ability to understand how letters and sounds come together to make words. Creating rhymes, completing stories, and substituting letters to create word chains (e.g., cat > hat > hit > bit) are simple activities with lots of depth for this age group.

In effect, the goal is to move beyond phonics—the sounds letters make—and putting sounds together as words. Ideally, children will cease to see words as individual letters and instead automatically process the text into words without having to think about it. This is one of the most difficult things for adults to remember about being a child. The act of reading is automatic for us. We see a word and read it without thinking. A child still has to work through this process.

While books and stories remain the dominant material that a child "reads," it is also important to consider nontraditional forms of reading material, particularly as many games require reading. Any exposure to written words is an opportunity for a child to practice reading. Specific guidelines on developing e-books and supporting children who are learning to read are discussed in chapter 20.

Kids often show a preference for a type of story or characters. They may love rhymes and silly stories or books about dinosaurs. While it is important that a child be exposed to lots of different kinds of words and stories, it is also important to provide a positive experience around literacy. If kids have a bad experience with literacy around this age, it can be very hard to undo.

Writing and Written Communication
By this age, kids have largely settled into which hand will be dominant, and their handwriting begins to stabilize and become legible. They are learning to write upper- and lower-case letters as well as to write with print and cursive letters. Simultaneously, they are generally learning to type.

As their confidence in writing increases, kids also grow in their ability to share their ideas in writing and to practice communicating. They make frequent spelling errors or spell phonetically, but they take great joy in sharing their stories. Their ability to write more detailed and longer stories varies greatly depending on their experiences with printed language. If their school and caregivers emphasize writing and exposure to different texts, they will likely expand their abilities accordingly.

Mathematical Thinking

Six-year-olds are mastering counting to higher and higher numbers as they learn the pattern for how to count. By age 7, they can count to 200, if not higher, though they're still learning to count backward reliably as well as to count by groups of numbers, such as counting by tens. Number lines are a common tool for this age, and children are learning to answer questions such as "What number comes before 42?"

Kids this age are also growing in their ability to estimate quantities as well as space (e.g., near, far). They are also using formal terms such as "greater than," "equal to," or "less than," as well as understanding when a number is "more" than another (e.g., 65 is more than 62).

They can write numbers in numeric form (1, 2, 3) as well as recognize the words for numbers (one, two, three). Performing addition and subtraction mentally still requires practice. They are additionally developing skills to answer word-based math problems without simply counting out objects. When asked to add two apples and three oranges, a younger child would physically create a group of three and a group of two and then count the entire group. An older child may still create a group of two and then "count on" to add three more by saying something like "one, two, plus three, four, and five."

Figure 11.3 *Dragon Shapes* provides kids with challenges to build by combining and rotating geometric shapes.

Dragon Shapes image used with permission of Lighthouse Learning.

While kids are largely familiar with basic geometric shapes, six-year-olds begin combining shapes to make other shapes as well as breaking apart more complex shapes into simpler parts. They also enjoy finding hidden shapes inside other pictures, such as those made popular by Hidden Pictures or tangrams. They continue to improve in their ability to use geometric shapes to construct other shapes well into their teen years.

Evidence of higher-order thinking, such as that required for algebra, can also be seen in children around ages 6–8. They begin to recognize patterns for solving math problems and may use those patterns as strategies for solving problems. They also improve at their ability to identify and complete patterns with three or more items.

Motor Skills

By age 7, kids have learned most motor movements and start to shift to refining the skills. They've learned to walk and hold a pencil; now they have to develop speed and accuracy. Their ability to do so depends largely on how frequently they practice. A child who spends little time kicking a ball will not progress as quickly in the skill as a child who regularly practices.

Kids settle into a hand preference of using either the right or the left hand for most fine motor tasks. As they practice writing, their handwriting stabilizes and becomes more legible. Kids also can learn and perform complex movements, such as dance steps, and perform them in rhythm as well, which makes dance games such as *Just Dance* popular. They are also improving in their ability to control their body in making smaller movements.

They become more aware of their personal space and are learning to respect others' personal space. It's not uncommon to have to remind kids to take a step backward when they're really excited about something.

As previously mentioned, this is a common age for kids to begin playing organized sports, which introduces a number of additional skills and opportunities to practice coordination.

Social and Emotional Development

Children in elementary school are still enthusiastic about showing off their talents, just like younger children. But they are improving in their ability to manage their emotions and enthusiasm. So where a preschooler may become angry if a parent asks him to wait until the end of a phone call, a six- or seven-year-old is better equipped to recognize and handle the frustration that arises and wait until the proper time.

That said, children of this age still need a lot of practice with recognizing and managing emotions both in themselves and in others. Conflicts still arise over sharing and other interactions. Role playing continues to be an important part of how children practice negotiating social situations. Participating in sports teams allows children to practice social skills in a rule-based environment.

Children are also continuing to develop a sense of self, for physical characteristics as well as less tangible characteristics such as preferences and dislikes. A common activity in schools is to have children supply information about themselves, which may include physical descriptions as well as things they enjoy doing.

In elementary school, a child's social circle expands rapidly as he is exposed to peers and develops friendships within the classroom. Prior to formal schooling, a child's social circle consists mostly of a small group of peers and caregivers. As elementary kids form new friends, early preferences for friends of the same gender also begin to emerge.

Scientific Thinking

Although children may have been exposed to some science curriculum prior to elementary school, most schools formally introduce the scientific method early in elementary school. It may be called STEM or STEAM (science, technology, engineering, arts, and math), but it is curriculum related to the sciences. In recent years, interest in this area has expanded rapidly.

STEM education takes many forms, from formal exposure to scientific concepts such as photosynthesis to informal practices that simply seek to encourage kids to be curious about the world around us. As

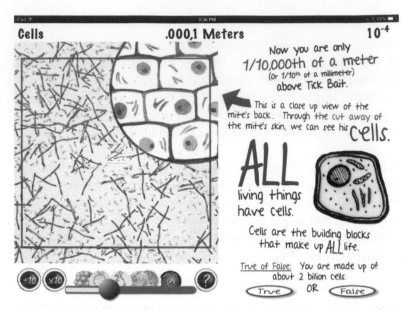

Figure 11.4 *Tick Bait's Universe* is an e-book that allows kids to zoom in and out of the world, allowing them to see things in microscopic detail all the way to a full view of the universe.

Tick Bait's Universe image used with permission of You University Apps.

early elementary kids are beginning to better separate make-believe from reality, a main focus of STEM education is to encourage kids to observe their environment and begin to investigate questions that interest them.

Games provide numerous opportunities to reinforce STEM concepts. For example, they might help children practice practical concepts, such as basic engineering, as well as abstract concepts that are hard to demonstrate in real life through simulations or e-books. For example, *Tick Bait's Universe* is a playful e-book that allows a child to zoom in and out of the world, allowing her to see the world from the molecular level all the way to the view from space.

Music and Creative Arts

Many children begin formal music training early in elementary school, often as piano or violin lessons. They can begin to learn to read music and to move in time with a beat. When they sing, they can generally sing the correct pitches and follow the basic contours of the song.

They enjoy creating artwork in both two-dimensional and three-dimensional forms. The art they create often reflects their personal lives, such as drawings of their family or pets. Storytelling apps and games are particularly popular with this age group, especially when it enables sharing with friends and family in a controlled, safe way.

Example Games for Early Elementary Kids

When kids enter elementary school, they begin their formal schooling, but they also begin to explore their ability to make choices for themselves. One way they can exercise their independence is in their choice of media they enjoy. While they may play educational games in school, they start to transition to casual entertainment content in their free time.

Social interactions around games such as *Club Penguin*, *Minecraft*, or *Moshi Monsters* often center on virtual worlds. Kids also frequently play casual games that are designed for all ages, such as *Cut the Rope*

Figure 11.5 As players solve puzzles in *Slice Fractions*, they are introduced to the concepts of fractions.

Slice Fractions image used with permission of Ululab.

or *Plants vs Zombies*. This makes it harder for developers, who are now competing with a pool of games much larger than just the pool of educational games.

Kids also begin to show preferences consistent with gender, as girls tend toward dress-up and caregiver-type games.

CHAPTER 12
Tweens (Ages 9–12)

Tweens are transitioning out of childhood and into the teen years. They can vary wildly in maturity. Their mood swings can be just as varying.

This chapter discusses the developmental milestones of children ages 9–12, including:

- An overview of their cognitive development
- Language and communication skills
- Mathematical thinking
- Motor skill development
- Social and emotional development
- Developmentally appropriate games for this age

Figure 12.1 Image used under Creative Commons Attribution License by Flickr member woodleywonderworks.

Developmental Milestones

Tweens improve rapidly in their ability to remember and recall information. This is attributed to the increased speed at which their brain can respond, their larger knowledge base about information they are trying to remember, and their acquisition of strategies specific to remembering things.

As for their entertainment choices, tweens generally stop watching "children's" programming and replace it with casual and family programming. This is true of their game choices as well.

Language and Communication

As tweens, kids are becoming independent readers, thinkers, and communicators. Expectations surrounding their ability to communicate turn to a refinement of skills needed to evaluate texts and communicate appropriately in writing—with proper spelling and writing—as well as in conversation.

Mathematical Thinking

Tweens also continue their acquisition of mathematical skills, moving into more complex forms of arithmetic (e.g., long division, fractions) and geometric thinking. Some at this age are introduced to formal algebra and basic statistics. *Dragon Box Algebra* is a frequently cited game for helping kids learn algebraic concepts. As the player completes levels, the game transitions into equation-based problems. However, even games that are less concrete about specific math skills, such as *TwoDots* or *Threes*, are valuable for reinforcing mathematical thinking.

Motor Skills

Tweens continue to improve in their motor skills, given time and support to practice. Boys tend to be a little stronger and faster than girls, while girls tend to be more agile. As they become teenagers, these differences become more pronounced.

Social and Emotional Development

Tweens spend nearly half of their time with peers and so the influence of adults becomes less direct. The majority of tweens will have a same-gender best friend as well. Cliques and small groups of friends emerge in school situations. Bullying and peer pressure also start to present a challenge to tweens.

As tweens are increasing in their ability to understand the motivations of actions, they also begin to practice moral reasoning. Understanding that a person can feel one way but act another requires the ability to deal with complex ideas.

This is also the start of puberty, so emotions can change rapidly, shifting from one extreme to another. Skills for managing and recognizing emotions remain an important focus.

Example Games for Tweens

Tweens are fully exploring their identity and social interactions as they begin to transition into adulthood. They are unlikely to choose to play an educational game on their own unless it is presented in a school setting. Many games, such as *Dance Dance Revolution* (physical activity, rhythm) or *Minecraft* (social interactions, engineering), however, are educational or beneficial in other, nontraditional ways. Games that foster STEM thinking, particularly for girls, are also common for this age group.

Figure 12.2 *MinecraftEdu* is an educational version of Minecraft, which includes tools for teachers to make assignments and manage multiple players. Even without the educational add-ons, the game is wildly popular with kids.

Image used with permission of Teacher Gaming LLC.

Figure 12.3 *Toca Hair Salon* and its sequels are popular with tween girls.
Image used with permission of Toca Boca AB.

Just as gender plays a significant role in tweens' social circles, gender also plays a large role in the types of games tweens play; boys tend to prefer racing games and first-person shooters, and girls tend to choose more social and caregiving games. *Toca Hair Salon* is a popular game with tween girls.

Tweens play a large number of casual games, on consoles and on handheld devices. They are as likely to play a game based on a familiar television show as they are to play a game that is based on new intellectual property.

CHAPTER 13
Teens (Ages 13+)

For the purposes of game design, teens are basically adults who are lacking a lot of life experience. They are able to reason and plan ahead, and they are also actively exploring their identities.

This chapter briefly discusses the developmental milestones of teens, including developmentally appropriate games for this age.

Figure 13.1 Image used under Creative Commons Attribution License by Flickr member Carissa Rogers.

Developmental Milestones

While this book is focused on children under the age of 12, for the purposes of providing a full developmental psychology picture, we offer a brief overview of teenagers.

Teens can solve problems by breaking them down into parts, and they take ethical and moral considerations into account as well. They are capable of logical thought and can understand abstract ideas.

Teens stand out from children in their ability to reason hypothetically and plan ahead. They're not perfect at it, but they are engaging in this kind of thinking, particularly about the consequences of their actions, more often than earlier in childhood. They also test conventional limits. Rather than simply follow the status quo, they may question why and test whether there is another way to do things.

In language and math, teens continue to advance in their knowledge, depending on their school experiences and preferences. They also continue the social expansion that started as tweens. Adult guidance is less direct as teens spend increased time with friends. Teens are particularly known for homophily in their friendships, which is the idea that their friends are very similar to themselves in terms of traits and behaviors.

Teens explore sexual relationships as well as take risks, socially and with drugs, during adolescence. Peer pressure and bullying are ongoing challenges for teens.

Their relationships with parents can be very strained during the teen years, particularly because teens feel caught between the need for independence and their need to continue to rely on their parents for many things.

Example Games for Teens

Because teens encounter numerous moral dilemmas, a number of developers create games that help introduce information and provide intervention for at-risk behaviors. These tend to fall into the category of

Figure 13.2 *Start the Talk* is a game that lets parents practice conversations around alcohol before actually talking about it with kids.

Image used with permission of Substance Abuse and Mental Health Services Administration and Kognito.

serious games and cover a wide range of topics. While not a game for teens per se, *Start the Talk* is a game that lets parents practice talking with kids about the dangers of alcohol abuse.

Beyond special topics, teens tend to play games that adults would play, including popular casual games and independent games such as *Gone Home*. Many teens play games that are rated for mature audiences, such as games from the *Grand Theft Auto* franchise, which can create tension between caregivers and teens.

An unusual game for teens and adults is *Zombies, Run!* It is a mobile game about outrunning zombies. The player listens to the audio narration while moving (preferably running), and success in the game is driven by how quickly the player moves. The game also tracks statistics about the player's runs.

Foldit is a game in which players contribute to scientific research by playing the game. It was developed at the University of Washington to explore the structure of proteins and to test whether humans' problem-solving and pattern-recognition skills are more efficient than those of computer software.

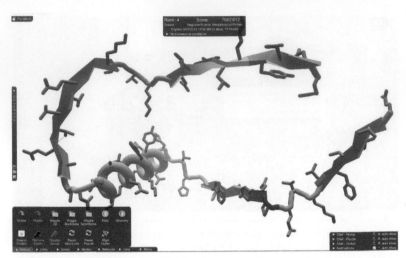

Figure 13.3 By solving levels in *Foldit*, players contribute to scientific research.

Image used with permission of University of Washington.

CHAPTER 14
Public Perceptions of Games for Kids

Beyond the challenge of creating developmentally appropriate content and engaging game mechanics with high production value, designers must also be aware of societal concerns around children's use of digital media.

Every few months, a new study provides additional data showing that children are using screen media for significant chunks of time at younger and younger ages. The research indicates that children are using technology quite frequently, and observers are raising a number of concerns about what this means for developing minds. Developers need to be aware of these issues and be prepared to talk about their views, as questions will undoubtedly arise from parents, teachers, and press.

The American Academy of Pediatrics (AAP) has long maintained that children under age 2 should not be exposed to screen media, including televisions and tablets. It recommends very limited exposure for children above age 2. In 2013, it updated the guidelines to reflect the reality that many children are exposed to screen media. The AAP still discourages screen media use for children under age 2. For older children, it recommends that parents limit screen time to one or two hours a day, establish media-free zones (e.g., no television in the bedroom), and co-view with children to help establish healthy media habits. Parents are encouraged to model appropriate media viewing behaviors.

Beyond the recommendations of organizations such as the AAP, concerns about children's use of media tend to center on the displacement of other activities by media consumption and worries that media are linked to an increase in violent behaviors.

Violence and Media

Entire volumes can be (and have been) written on the topic of violence and media. It's well beyond the scope of this book to review the arguments, but at a general level parents, educators, policy makers, and researchers are all concerned that exposure to violent content influences children to act in violent ways. The exposure may come via games, movies, or the news, but the concern is that children may become desensitized to violence because of it.

The research is mixed and very politically charged. If you're making content that could be perceived as violent—even cartoon violence—it's important to spend time crafting how you will address concerns about your product.

When I'm asked, I tend to say something like the following:

It will be years before we know the impact of violent media on children (or on humans in general). Common sense, however, tells us that kids should not play a game that they are not developmentally, socially, or emotionally ready for.

Therefore, everyone has a responsibility to make sure that kids play only games that are suited for them. That means that game studios must label and market their games accordingly. Similarly, parents and educators need to take an active role overseeing what children play. They need to familiarize themselves with rating systems and review sites and play content in advance or with their children to make sure it's appropriate. Additionally, parents should help children find games and other activities that are related to their interests and help replace their media content if something appears to be too scary for their child.

Displacement of Activities with Media

Many parents and teachers worry that other children's activities are displaced because children spend so much time viewing screen media such as television and games. Usually the concern is raised that kids aren't spending enough time outside or that they aren't reading as much. Time is zero-sum; there are only 24 hours in a day, and so doing one activity logically displaces something else.

When I speak to this concern, I stress the importance of selecting a variety of activities in which to participate in moderation as well as the need to select quality content. Providing a variety of experience is key to raising a child in general. Kids learn from every experience, and we want them to experience a wide range of activities in moderation to learn best.

The concern with displacement of activities comes when children experience media in large quantities. Almost any activity in extreme amounts will lead to trouble, be it eating 5,000 calories of chocolate a day or eating 5,000 calories of broccoli a day. Similarly, a heavy diet of screen media isn't the best thing for anyone at any age. Moderation and variety are key, and parents and educators are the gatekeepers.

Additionally, we no longer need to consider media as a whole experience but rather evaluate it according to the content and genres within it. Watching romantic comedies is going to result in different information being passed to the viewer than watching documentaries. What content we choose for children is important for their experiences. Encouraging content that is age appropriate, thoughtfully designed, or based on research is a far better option.

Common sense is again very important. Additionally, as a developer, you can help caregivers select the right content by clearly communicating any research, curriculum standards, advisers, or other development tools used to create the product. The appendix includes a number of places where developers can get information on the most recent research findings.

Developing Media Specifically for Children under Age 5

The concerns already mentioned apply to media consumption in general. Developing screen media (e.g., television, games) for children under age 2 and even for children under age 5 can be controversial for additional reasons; some are for it, some are against it, and some are in the middle. If you are considering making a product for very young children, familiarize yourself with the various arguments before making a jump into the space.

In part, the concern is that researchers have yet to fully understand the impact of screen media. With limited information, professionals making recommendations for screen media consumption by young children tend to err on the side of caution. But that fails to acknowledge the reality of being a parent.

Most parents use screen media at some point with young children, often simply for a few minutes' distraction while the parent takes a shower or makes dinner. But if you talk to parents who use screen media out of necessity, the overwhelming majority of them express guilt for doing so.

When I'm asked specifically about technology and young children, especially those under age 2, my answer is that parents have to arm themselves with all the information they can and then make the decision that's right for them. The choice of what's an appropriate amount of screen time for your child, as well as what that screen time will consist of, is intensely personal, as are most parenting decisions. Some decide that TV is fine, especially when they're trying to put dinner on the table. Others steer clear of screens completely.

I often refer parents to a set of guidelines issued in 2012 by the National Association for the Education of Young Children and the Fred Rogers Center for Early Childhood Learning and Children's Media. Their joint statement is titled "Technology and Interactive Media as Tools in Early Childhood Programs Serving Children from Birth through Age 8."

In the statement, which is developed for educators but is also helpful for parents to consider, the authors acknowledge the conflicting evidence on the value of technology in children's lives. They also wisely acknowledge that not all screens are created equal. The paper covers a broad range of ideas for approaching technology with children, but they boil it down to six recommendations, two of which are relevant to this discussion:

> Recommendation #3: Prohibit the passive use of television, videos, DVDs, and other non-interactive technologies and media in early

childhood programs for children younger than 2, and discourage passive and non-interactive uses with children ages 2 through 5.

Recommendation #4: Limit any use of technology and interactive media in programs for children younger than 2 to those that appropriately support responsive interactions between caregivers and children and that strengthen adult-child relationships.

("Technology and Interactive Media," 11)

Basically, the statement recognizes that recommendations call for no screen time for children under age 2 but acknowledges that almost all parents use some amount of screen media with their young children. Instead of making anyone feel guilty about that, the authors found a way to walk the line between what research tells us and the realities of being a parent, particularly by differentiating between passive and interactive screen time.

In other words, if a child is going to be exposed to a screen at a young age, it should be an interactive experience that adult and child can do together.

This creates a number of opportunities for developers. For example, you might decide to foster parent/child discussion through cooperative play. Whether it's making predictions of what's going to happen or stopping to talk about what we just did, every moment, not just with technology, is an opportunity to draw connections to other things. We discuss cooperative game design in chapter 21.

Depending on the age of the child, you can also encourage parents and kids to make their own games together. Or you can provide supplemental materials that help the parent extend the game into their offline experiences. For example, if they're working on letters, include suggestions on finding the letters in the real world ("Look for the letter A on boxes at the grocery store!").

Additionally, carefully craft your marketing and packaging materials. The act of simply making content for young children brings a lot of scrutiny. A number of watchdog organizations will publicly call out a company that makes broad, sweeping promises about the educational value of its products. (Google "Your Baby Can Read," or "Fisher-Price and Open Solutions" to see a few examples of what can happen.) In chapter 23 we discuss how to market your games.

CHAPTER 15
User Testing with Kids

User testing (or play testing) is an enlightening experience that should be included throughout the design process. Additionally, testing should be done directly with kids whenever possible to gather the most useful information. It's unfair to expect parents or other adults to know how kids will react to programs, both in terms of the appeal of the game and the way in which it is used. By directly observing children using your program several times throughout design, you can avoid problems and continually develop your own intuition on how kids play.

Many design teams opt to perform user testing with a professional firm that specializes in testing. While effective, this can be very expensive. Professional freelance testers are generally more affordable and should be able to help with all aspects, including designing the research, recruiting, performing the research itself, and summarizing the findings.

This chapter will guide you through the testing process. Even if you are planning to use a professional tester, this chapter will help familiarize you with what to expect. If you're performing the testing yourself, this chapter can also serve as a guide to establish your own process.

What Needs to Be Tested?

When it comes to user testing, the complaints I hear are generally true—it's a lot of work, expensive, and time consuming. User testing takes a lot of resources to do properly, but it pays off in the end. The challenge is determining how to best direct the resources to get the most out of the experience. I use these questions to focus on which areas and features to test.

1. Has someone else designed a similar product or feature? In this crowded marketplace, it's entirely likely that you're not the first person to design a particular feature set, even if it doesn't look exactly the same as in another game. By being familiar with lots of games, you'll likely find designs that are similar to yours in one way or another. This can provide valuable information on how to best implement the design. You might also use these other products to do initial testing before you start spending your own design and research resources.

2. Is there research available on your particular designs and features? While the first question focuses on what has been designed, it's also possible that particular interactions and design features have been researched but not widely distributed as a commercial product. This is particularly true in educational technology, where researchers frequently test ideas for the purposes of improving education. Academic journals and conferences are a great source for exploring additional research on products that were not released commercially. The appendix includes some examples of resources for this information.

3. Is there research in related areas that would be useful? I also try to look at research in similar areas to see if there's anything relevant that might inform the testing. For example, when I first started developing for stylus-based interactions, I also looked at research on how children hold pencils and learn to write. That helped me understand that they use varying grips and pressure and that their accuracy is refined over time. This knowledge in turn helped guide our considerations of tracing activities and of target sizes.

4. Judging from your experience (or that of colleagues and advisors), what are the areas or interactions in your game that are innovative or risky? Only a few projects can afford to test everything. You have to trust your gut and focus on the things you're worried about. If

another problem surfaces during the testing, then you can readjust. So take a hard look at your product and focus on the spots that are likely to be a problem.

Another way to start to zero in on problem areas is to watch a few people play the current version of the game. That may provide enough information to focus the test further.

When Does Testing Happen?

The timing of play testing varies from studio to studio and project to project. I prefer to start testing as soon as possible. But it also depends on whether the game is breaking new ground, perhaps because of new hardware, features, interaction patterns, or game mechanics.

When I'm designing a project that is more experimental, I definitely start testing as soon as possible. For example, when I was creating *Stride & Prejudice*, an endless runner where an avatar runs across scrolling horizontal text, I started testing the game with a very crude prototype. I didn't even know if other people would think the idea was funny or interesting as a game.

By the time *Stride & Prejudice* launched, more than 200 people had played the game and given me feedback. This led to changes in features and a lot of tuning of the game.

When I'm designing a project that's largely understood, such as an e-book for the iPad, testing still happens but not as often. We still identify the risk areas, such as new mini games within the game, and

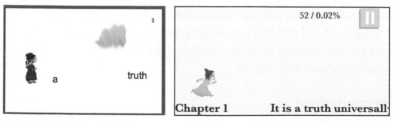

Figures 15.1–15.2 An early prototype of *Stride & Prejudice* and the final design.

Images used with the permission of No Crusts Interactive.

test those early. Otherwise, we'll likely do tests at alpha and beta to make sure that everything is holding together well. That, of course, introduces the risk of having to make changes late in the development cycle if we find a major issue.

For peace of mind, then, it's really better as a rule to get feedback, but when you have to manage a budget, new features, technology, or interactions that you haven't worked with before or when you do not have research on how kids use the technology, testing should happen as soon as possible.

What about People Stealing Ideas?

Whenever I make the statement that people should test early and test often, someone asks about how to protect your idea from being stolen. Theft is a risk, and you do need to be smart about not showing off your secret sauce to every random person.

Ideas are easy, but executing the idea is hard. So, while people may be interested in your idea, they probably have many of their own ideas that are a higher priority for them. By conducting testing, you are helping to ensure that the execution of your idea is flawless. However, if you are truly concerned about theft, show your game only to people you trust or people who are recommended by people you trust.

Remember that you're also showing the game to your target audience. Kids aren't likely to steal your idea!

On occasion, a developer will request the testers to fill out a nondisclosure agreement. Keep in mind that any sort of legal document can be intimidating to parents who are not familiar with the technology industry. It's okay to state that the materials they are seeing are in development and that you would appreciate their not discussing what they see, but anything more formal than that is likely to turn parents away before they even sign up.

Recruitment

Finding kids can be a challenge for testing, especially if you're not a parent. You can use a variety of recruitment methods, depending on how formal a test you desire. If you work with a professional market research firm, it will handle recruitment. But the firms are expensive, so you can try other options.

Ask colleagues or friends who have kids to try out the game. If you are testing informally, have the parent bring the child to the office (or go to their home) so that you can see the child play. Facebook is another tool for reaching friends, as well as asking friends to spread the word that you are looking for testers.

Approach local schools or afterschool programs and inquire about testing there. Developing a relationship with a school principal or teachers can take a long time. Some schools also have strict rules on when and how they can participate in these kinds of activities. Proceed cautiously, and know that it may take multiple tries to find the right school.

A number of neighborhood communities have parenting e-mail lists. This is particularly true in urban areas. Search online, as many of these groups use online tools such as MeetUp and are publicly listed.

Once you start building connections, be sure to nurture and maintain the relationships. This way you have a resource to draw on whenever you have testing needs. Reach out personally to particularly valuable connections to maintain goodwill. Many kids and parents are genuinely excited to participate in the process of game development. You can build additional goodwill by offering to speak at schools or clubs about your career, or you can invite a few students to shadow you for a day. This helps them feel they are part of a community and not simply being used as testers.

Sample Size

The question of exactly how many kids should play your game to give you ample feedback is tough to answer. If you are involved in formal evaluation and research, the sample size will be dictated by the need to create a statistically significant sample. But in most commercial situations your goal will simply be to test with as many kids as your budget can handle.

The kinds of questions you're answering will also inform how many data points you need. If you are performing a survey to find out the media habits of average children or what kinds of programs they like to watch, then you need a lot of kids. If you want to know if a product helps kids learn a particular skill, you'll need a lot of kids within the target demographic. If you want to know if your interface is usable, then you can get by with fewer testers.

When I'm testing the usability of a product, I like to get at least four kids of each age (and mixed gender) to play. So, for example, if I'm developing a game for four- to seven-year-olds, then I want at least 16 kids—four each of four-year-olds, five-year-olds, six-year-olds, and seven-year-olds. If demographic factors such as ethnicity or family income are important, then you may need to add more kids.

Often my initial research provides more than enough information for me to proceed. But sometimes it introduces a question that could be considered a problem or simply something to keep an eye on. When this happens, I try to get additional users to play the game as soon as possible.

Permissions to Test and Record

Whenever you are testing with children, you should ask for permission from the parents. But some situations require more than a courteous request.

If your project is part of an academic research study (e.g., one funded by a government agency or one whose results you plan to publish in an academic journal), then you are required to have permission from an institutional review board (IRB). This is an ethical review board that makes sure your project is treating subjects fairly and humanely. The primary investigators on your project should be familiar with this process and will explain the requirements, which can be quite involved.

Schools generally require that the classroom teacher as well as parents agree to the testing in writing. Some schools may also require you to pass their own IRB process, even if the research is solely for internal development purposes.

Even if you aren't subject to review by an institutional review board, it is ethical to inform your users and their parents of what the testers will be asked to do and to mitigate any risks. You can do this in an age-appropriate way, but you should let parents and kids know what the kids will be looking at and whether there are any risks involved (such as being out of breath from an exercise game) and also remind them that the kids do not have to complete the testing and that if they become uncomfortable, they can stop at any time.

If you are developing games and performing research for commercial purposes, then you should still seek permission from the parents. As part of the permission letter, you can ask for permission to record or photograph the child if you plan to share the results in a presentation or with anyone beyond your immediate team.

Incentives

It's common to thank both parent and child for participating in the research. Parents might receive a monetary compensation. Depending on the age, kids could be given a coloring book, t-shirt, game, or gift certificate. It's often against rules to compensate a teacher directly, so some organizations make a donation to the school in exchange for participation. In general, you should check local laws or rules that might affect what you use as incentives for participation.

Testing with Parents versus Kids

Recruiting kids for testing can be difficult, so there's a clear temptation to simply talk to the parents. Parents are unlikely to have all the information you need. They can probably speak to the child's content preferences and what devices the child owns (though you'd be surprised how many parents actually don't know!).

The major reason for performing user testing, however, is to make sure your game is usable by the target audience. Parents can't tell you if their child will understand the instructions or navigate the game levels easily. When your questions are focused on usability, focus on testing with the target audience.

Testing at Home or School versus Lab-Based Research

Performing research at the child's home or school provides a natural picture of how the child will interact with the game, including the presence of distractions. Testing in a lab or office setting provides a more focused set of information, but kids may also be on their best behavior.

Whether a natural setting (home or school) or a lab setting (office or a research facility) is right for you depends on the questions you are studying. Do you need the rich data, or are you focused on the playability of your game?

If you are interested in how children play console games in their living room, then performing the research in the home of lots of kids is relevant. If you are testing the usability of your product, then a lab setting will be appropriate.

Performing the Research

It sometimes seems that the actual research days are the hardest, as kids can be quite a handful to manage. But there are a number of things you can do in advance to make sure you get the most out of the day.

Set Up the Testing Environment for the Child

If you are working in a lab setting, prepare the room for the child. Remove distractions. (White boards and markers are especially tempting, I've discovered!)

I adjust the room for the child as much as possible, especially if we're testing on computers. For example, I make sure the computer monitor is at the child's eye height and not at the height appropriate for an adult. Sometimes we bring a child-size computer mouse, too. We're testing the usability of our interface, not the usability of the computer setup and hardware. If you cannot test in the setting in which your game will be used, try to make the testing environment as similar as possible to the target environment.

Overbook Sessions to Allow for Choice

If you have the luxury of too many participants, some researchers overbook sessions and then select the happiest and/or most talkative children.

Recruit Pairs of Friends

When you're testing with small groups of kids, ask the recruited child to bring a friend along. This provides an extra child for your research. The children are also likely to be more comfortable with someone familiar around and will speak more freely.

When Should Parents Sit In on the Testing?

When you're testing with really young children, the parents should always be in the room. The child will feel more secure, and the parent can also help translate what the child is saying. (Toddlers can be hard to understand.)

Around age 4 or so, some kids will participate in the research alone. Ask the child and parent whether they want to be together. As mentioned, parents are useful for translating what children say. The parent-child dynamic can also be really helpful for understanding how they prompt the child to finish a task. You can gain valuable insight on how to phrase instructions by watching parents.

The downside of having parents in the room is that they may interject their thoughts or overprompt the child. I usually tell parents to interact with the child as they would at home. If the parent is interfering too much, I gently mention that I'm really interested in what the child has to say. Most parents will take the hint!

Recognize When It's Just Better to End the Session

Kids are kids, which means you will get tears, temper tantrums, running around, nose picking, throw-up, potty accidents, and a host of other crazy events. Prepare yourself in advance that some sessions will not yield useful information.

Encourage Team Members to Watch Sessions

Some testing environments are set up so that team members can watch sessions, either behind a one-way mirror or via a video feed. I encourage team members to watch at least some user testing sessions as it's a great opportunity to see kids in action, but it comes with risks as well.

Team members who have not watched a lot of testing may feel uncomfortable or even defensive when they hear criticism of their product. They may also make snap decisions based on a single user rather than wait to see the full results of all sessions.

If the team was consulted in the creation of the testing goals, it will at least know what features are being examined and have a sense of what to expect in the session. We regularly discuss what we see in the testing as it's happening or shortly thereafter, but I keep an eye out for decisions that are being made on the basis of single data points. If I feel a recommendation is being made in haste, I'll recommend that we make a note of it and keep watching to see how the rest of the sessions proceed.

Whenever possible, I take note of the concerns, and then we regroup and discuss everything once we have all the data at the end of the testing. The exception to this is if we find a bug during testing that negatively impacts playing the game, such as a crash bug, which we fix as soon as possible.

Designing the Test Sessions

Designing the testing session is as important as the actual testing session. Without advanced planning, you run the risk of wasting time and collecting data that's not valuable.

Define Your Testing Goals

While some testing sessions are for exploratory purposes—you go in to see what happens and where problems might pop up—the majority of user testing sessions have a specific purpose. The more specific you can be about that purpose, the more useful the sessions will be.

If you approach testing like traditional research, your goal will be to answer questions or address a hypothesis. Is my game usable? Do the players understand the instructions? Where do they get stuck? Can they navigate from the game to the options area and get back into the game?

Exercises in designing research questions can be useful for team communication as well. Team members may express concerns about particular features or functionality more easily when discussing what to research. If you're using a professional moderator, the research questions will also help the moderator become familiar with the product and your priorities.

If you're performing the testing yourself, specific questions will help you maintain objectivity and focus. As you can likely imagine, putting your work in front of people to critique can be nerve-wracking, even when your testers are adorable four-year-olds. There is always an immense temptation to rationalize or ignore feedback that indicates that you need to change direction or improve on the design, especially if you're performing the testing yourself.

Validity versus Reliability

Reliability is the degree to which testers achieve consistent results if given a test more than once. This is particularly important when you have more than one person performing the user testing. If two user testers watch the same video of a child playing a game, will they provide the same feedback? Do both people judge the same way? When a test is reliable, it means your testing methods are sound enough to be used consistently many times.

During informal testing, you often want varied opinions, and so you may not be very concerned with reliability so long as you have one person who ultimately filters all the feedback. At other times, such as when you're evaluating a game on its ability to teach a particular skill, you want to be as certain as possible that the reviewers are trained to evaluate the sessions in the same way. In research, this is referred to as interrater reliability.

Validity indicates that your test actually measures what you think it is measuring. If you step on the scale to weigh yourself, you trust that the scale is a valid measurement of your weight. If it's off by two pounds, it's no longer a valid tool. When you're testing games, testing with an audience of different ages creates a problem with validity. If you use a ten-year-old to get feedback on your game for three-year-olds, the feedback is not necessarily valid. Validity is particularly tricky when a game has educational goals. You need to assess whether progress in your game is a valid measure of learning. Just because they learn letter names in your game does not mean that a child will be able to name letters on a standardized literacy measurement tool. Similarly, if you ask a child if she is learning and she says yes, it doesn't mean that she is learning—it means only that she thinks she is learning. That's an important distinction in assessing the validity of the test.

One more place to watch for validity is on survey data. Surveys often rely on a person's memory to answer questions such as "How much television did you watch yesterday?" People are not very good at estimating time spent on a task, and they get even worse when the event is farther in the past (yesterday versus last week versus last month). So the validity of their responses is in question. Additionally, people may respond to questions with answers that they think are correct or that reflect what they think they should do. Parents will overreport how many books they have in the house or how often they read to their kids.

So this is a word of caution when you're designing your user testing sessions: keep an eye on validity and reliability. If you're in doubt, ask a colleague who specializes in testing to review your research protocol and provide feedback.

Set the Tone

Once you're in the session with the child, set the tone and explain how the session will go. I like to tell the child that since he's an expert in playing games, I need his help to make the game better. Everyone likes to feel empowered and welcome to share thoughts freely, right?

I then explain that we're going to play games together and that the child can share any thoughts, even if he or she doesn't like the game. (Kids are often coached to tell you only positive things.) If we're using a prototype, I explain that some parts of the game may not work properly. Finally, I share that the child can leave at any time.

Allow Time to Play

It's tempting to program the entire session with nonstop questions that help you get the answers you need, but this generally leads to an unhappy child. We find that a balance between free play and focused time to answer questions is a great balance. Like grown-ups, kids will tolerate questions and focused effort if they will have time to have fun in a few minutes.

Session Lengths

How long the sessions should be depends, in part, on what you're testing and with what methods. But as a rule of thumb, the younger the child, the shorter the session should be. Aim for 20–30 minutes for children under age 6 and 30–45 minutes for older children.

Develop a Research Protocol

Having a document that details the research protocol, or how the research sessions will proceed, is useful for numerous reasons. In particular, it helps you focus on your goals and efficiently manage time in the session. It also increases consistency among those moderating the testing sessions.

The research protocol can be a simple list of questions, or it can be a multiple-page document of questions. This is a sample protocol.

Hi, [Name of child]! I'm [Researcher Name], and today we're going to play a game that I've been working on with some friends. I hear you like to play games? [Pause]

What kinds of games do you play? [Probe for additional games/platforms as needed.]

That's great! Well, in a moment I'll show you the game! Since you play so many games, I'm really curious to hear what you think, even if you don't like the game. By playing today, you'll help us make a better game that lots of kids like you can enjoy. When we're finished, you'll have time to play, too.

[Open game] So this is [Game Name]. How about you give it a try? [Let child play for five to seven minutes.]

[If child appears stuck or asks for help, prompt child to talk out loud about things he can try.]

[Once child has finished playing, ask the following questions.]

So what did you do in the game?

What did you think?

Who is this game for? [If child is unsure, alternate question is "Who would you tell about this game?"]

[If appropriate, remind child about a moment where he was stuck in the game and prompt for more information.]

Is there anything else you'd like to tell me about this game?

Thanks for playing with me today! If you'd like to play again, we have a few more minutes.

One of the most common mistakes researchers make when soliciting feedback from users is asking double-barreled questions, that is, asking two questions at once, making it impossible to answer with a single answer.

Double-barreled questions, like those here, are impossible to handle if a respondent wants to answer affirmatively to one part and negatively to the other.

- Which do you play: Nintendo Wii or Nintendo DS?
- Does your family enjoy adventure and puzzle games?
- Is this game fun and educational?

Also beware of asking questions that will lead to a false positive. For example, asking parents if they monitor their children's media use, they will usually be tempted to say yes. Parents know what they are supposed to do, which is to monitor their children, but the reality is that they do it far less often than they would like. It's very hard to admit the reality, especially in front of others. Asking people if they like a product can also result in similar false positives, as they're trying to be helpful and cooperative during the interviews.

Pilot Test Your Research

Before you book two days of testing sessions with kids, try out your research protocol and research questions on one or two kids. You may find that you planned too many questions for the available time or that some questions are confusing.

During the actual testing, you may find that your protocol needs to be adjusted, perhaps because of things you clarified along the way. This is generally okay unless you are in the midst of a large research study, in which case you should discuss any changes to the protocol with the team managers before proceeding.

Summarizing the Research

Once the research is happening, find moments to write down your notes as often as possible. I try to make notes in between sessions. If I don't, the people blur together and I lose some nuances that I wanted to consider more.

If the research is happening across multiple days, I also review my session notes and summarize them daily. If others are researching with me, we often debrief together as part of this process.

Once the research is complete, the entire team involved in the testing, including those who were observing the testing, should debrief, including reviewing their notes and sharing their takeaways. I often follow up with another meeting after the team has had time to think about the experience. During this meeting, which may be days or weeks later, we discuss how to implement the findings or what new questions emerged. In formal settings with professional moderators, a report summarizing the findings may also be created for the team.

User Testing Methods

This section describes a number of methods you might use in user testing your games. It's not an exhaustive list, but it covers many of the common options.

Focus Groups

When most people think about user testing, they usually think of focus groups. The participants sit around a table and tell a moderator what they think. Focus groups are particularly useful for gathering attitudes about a product or concept, but they are less useful for usability testing.

Preschool kids can theoretically participate in focus groups, but groups that include older kids who are able to sit still, listen, and express their opinions are easier to manage.

The risks of using a focus group include the possible presence of rowdy kids who don't want to sit still and what's known as "groupthink," a coalescing of voices around the dominant opinions. This happens when one or two people in the group are louder and more domineering than others and not everyone feels comfortable expressing opposing views.

The costs depend on the formality of the group and number of participants. Running focus groups in a professional setting is far more expensive than visiting a classroom and talking to kids.

Interviews

One-on-one interviews are great for assessing a person's understanding of a concept as well as for gathering people's individual preferences. As with most testing methods, the cost largely depends on the level of formality and the number of participants. Because you are talking to one person at a time, it takes far longer to collect data. At the same time, the data will be far richer.

Interviews vary greatly in structure. The entire session could be spent in conversation, working through a series of questions. Or it might involve a mix of time spent observing the player and talking to them about their experience.

The older the child, the easier the interview should be, as older kids are much better at expressing themselves. Younger kids, especially those under age 6, can be interviewed, but you have to be creative.

For example, you might have the child point to images of faces displaying emotions to explain how she feels about a game. When discussing the games, use screenshots to help the child remember specific experiences. "We played a game at this location today. What can you tell me about it?" Or ask the users to draw a picture of their experience and tell you about it. Grounding the conversation in a picture helps keep them focused.

But kids are still kids, so the quality of their answers will depend largely on their mood. I've been in many sessions where kids answer a question about the game by telling me about what they ate for lunch or singing a song. Patience and a sense of humor are needed to do interviews with kids.

Be creative with the questions you ask, too. It's tempting to ask kids "grown-up" questions, like "What age child is this game for?" Questions like this are too abstract for them to answer reliably. Instead, rephrase questions in ways kids can talk about, such as "Who is this game for? Your brother? Your friends?" or "Who would you tell about this game?"

Also avoid asking what game the testers liked best. No matter how many games they played, they will tell you the one they played most recently is their favorite. I've seen kids cry and express hatred for the last game. Then, five minutes later, they tell us it was their favorite. Until they're eight years old or even older, they just can't answer that question reliably!

Observations

When using observations in testing, the moderator provides the child with a task or game and then watches what happens. Observations are frequently paired with interviews to provide a rich picture of how kids play games and what they think of the experience. As with interviews, the cost depends on the formality of the session and the number of participants.

Observations can be done in one-on-one settings or they can be done in a group, where one or more moderators watch a number of children. Television research is often done this way; researchers observe a group of kids watching a television show and take note of particular behaviors.

Depending on the goals of the testing session, observations can be structured or unstructured. Unstructured observations have no goals or very loosely defined goals, and the moderator is simply watching to see what happens and noting potential areas for further study. In structured observations, the moderator is looking for a predefined set of behaviors, though she may also make notes of additional behaviors that are above and beyond the targeted behaviors.

Observed behaviors can be verbal or physical actions, including:
- Positive verbal utterances (e.g., "Hooray," "I did it!")
- Positive body language (e.g., dancing, jumping)
- Negative verbal utterances (e.g., sighs, "That was too hard")
- Negative body language (e.g., slumping, scrunching face)
- Closing the game
- Asking for help from a peer
- Asking for help from an adult
- Sharing progress with a peer
- Selecting a particular option
- Getting stuck in a particular place

The list of target behaviors has to be defined in advance and is often informed by earlier unstructured observations and the research questions. Some researchers also have screenshots of the software or prototypes that are being tested. Then, as the researchers observe notable behaviors, they make the notes on the relevant screenshot, rather than wasting time describing where the player was. Even a shorthand system for identifying areas can be helpful in this case, too.

Diaries

When you want to know more about the content and games children or families use at home, outside a lab setting, and/or how often they use the materials, diaries are a useful tool. The diary is a form that the family fills out over a period of time, noting data such as what television shows family members watch (and how long) or when they play games. It's very low cost but is not without challenges. The simplest form of a diary is a table with areas to track date, start time, end time, and behaviors of interest, such as what game was played and who was playing.

Diaries require the person to be old enough to be able to write, so it's best used with older kids or kids whose parent can be involved. It's also very easy for parents to forget to fill out the form, which generally leads to a diary that's filled in several days later on the basis of their memory of events rather than what actually happened. Rather than send home a paper document, consider using an online form, and then send regular e-mails to prompt the family to complete the diary.

Surveys

Like diaries, surveys are useful for finding out particular information about what kids play, how often they play it, and their attitudes. Surveys are easier to implement with children who are old enough to read and write, but it is possible to use surveys with younger children when the surveys are designed specifically with them in mind. In this case, design the survey so that the parent and child fill out the survey together. Rather than use words for the answers, use pictures, such as smiley faces to judge emotional response or characters and logos to judge familiarity with content.

Surveys cost little to implement, and a number of online tools make it very easy to design and collect information. As with all test methods, it's important to test out a survey in advance to make sure the questions are clearly written and easy to answer; avoid asking double-barreled questions.

Data Tracking

Tracking user behavior data has become quite common, especially now that a number of third-party tools are available to developers. A developer might track session lengths, number of sessions, or device used. It's also possible to track numerous factors, such as right and wrong answers, areas visited while playing the game, or places that users touch on the screen.

Data are useful for all ages of player. Tracking does not require players to express their thoughts verbally. The data are simply collected as the player plays the game.

Collecting data arbitrarily will not lead to great results. You need to have specific questions or goals in mind when you decide what information to track. Here are some ideas.

- Track how long users are spending in sessions. This way, when you make changes to the game, you can track the impact on session length. Did the new feature add to the length of time players spent in game?
- Track right and wrong answers across time so that you have an idea of whether the child is improving over time.
- Track where on the screen the child is tapping so that you know what objects the child is trying to tap on. This is useful for understanding what in the user interface the child thinks is clickable.

Sometimes the data identify situations that require additional investigation. For example, you might track where in the game users are spending time and display these patterns as a heat map. If you see users spending significantly more time in one area, this indicates that you should examine the area. Are users spending more time there because it's a fun activity? Is there a usability problem that's caused them to get stuck?

A/B testing is also tracked via automated data collection. In A/B testing, users are divided into groups that receive different experiences; later, data from both groups are compared. For example, group A might see a screen with bright orange colors, whereas group B sees a screen with warm orange colors. The point is to see which group spends more time on the site. If group B stays longer, then the team continues with that design and iterates further. The differences between the groups can be relatively simple or dramatically different.

With the availability of third-party tools, data tracking is far more affordable than it used to be. However, many developers find that their particular design needs require a custom system, which can be cost-prohibitive. If you are considering tracking user data, you have to think this through at the beginning of the project, because it is very difficult to engineer into a game after production has begun.

A significant consideration in tracking data, however, is whether your product must comply with any legal regulations for managing personalized data, such as COPPA, a U.S. law that governs what data can be collected from children. Before implementing any data tracking in your game, consult with a qualified professional to ensure that you are in compliance. Compliance can also include meeting local institutional requirements regarding data collection and the need to have people's consent before you can include them as part of the research.

User Testing Summary

User testing can be a daunting task to add to the production cycle, but it is an important part that will help you avoid costly mistakes and refine the product. Beyond this chapter, a number of resources (listed in the appendix) are available to help you design the research. Spending part of the budget on a professional moderator who can help design the protocol and recruit children will also make the process easier.

Sometimes user testing is simply too expensive for the budget. When that happens, be resourceful in finding kids to play the game even informally by asking friends and colleagues to try out the game. A number of cities host local game developer nights, where you can demo the game and receive feedback (and find people with kids to try out the game). Even a little testing goes a long way!

PART 3

Game Design Guidelines

Image used under Creative Commons Attribution License from Flickr member Thijs Knaap.

This section provides guidelines for the design and development of games for children. The chapters cover interaction design, scaffolding and tutorial design, educational versus commercial considerations, e-books, cooperative gameplay, and the incorporation of data into design. It ends with guidelines for marketing children's games.

CHAPTER 16
Best Practices

Regardless of what kind of game you design or what technology a child will use to play your game, there are general best practices for designing usable interfaces for kids.

This chapter discusses a number of best practices and production considerations for developers, including:

- Designing for a wide range of abilities
- Designing for quick or accidental success
- Designing games with multiple answer paths
- Using iconic, consistent design
- Creating large target hot spots
- Avoiding long, continuous movements
- Supporting a child learning to scroll through content
- Using vivid production to attract a child's attention
- Managing in-app purchases with gesture gates
- Limiting file size

Design for a Wide Range of Abilities

The most significant challenge facing game designers targeting children's audiences is the incredible range of abilities of any given target audience. Two four-year-olds can have wildly different skills and yet still qualify as "normal." To be commercially viable, children's games have to be designed to accommodate wide ranges of abilities.

At a practical level, this means your users will vary in their familiarity with how to play games and interact with technology. A child who picks up your game may be experiencing this genre of game, games in general, or even interactive technology for the very first time. The next child who picks up your game may have already played dozens of other games.

A number of games, most of which were not designed for children, have successfully accomplished this goal of designing for a wide

Figure 16.1 Dance games, such as *Dance Dance Revolution*, offer beginner levels that accommodate a young player as well as expert levels, which allow the game to be played by people with a wide range of abilities.

Image used under Creative Commons Attribution License by Flickr member Monterey Public Library.

range of abilities, whether they meant to or not. Two classic examples are *Dance Dance Revolution*, that lets you step in time to music on a dance mat, and *Wii Sports* a Nintendo title in which you use the Wii Remote to mimic basic sports motions. YouTube is filled with videos of young children playing these games along with teenagers, parents, and grandparents. *Dance Dance Revolution* is particularly notable for the level of expertise it supports, from complete novice to expert professional dancer. *The bowling game in Wii Sports* falls into the category of "simple to learn, difficult to master." The interaction requirements are so simple that an 18-month-old child can learn to play. Additionally, the game doesn't heavily penalize the player for being a novice.

Design for Accidental or Quick Success

Because of the wide range of choices available to them, kids are often quick to put down an experience if it is too difficult or confusing to use. While there are many aspects to designing a good and engaging game, the simplest instruction to remember is to design for quick success or accidental success. In other words, the child should be able to open the game and get into the gameplay experience within seconds.

The idea is to make it as clear and straightforward as possible for the child to start the experience. If they're left hunting around for what to do, they'll find the experience frustrating.

One example of very simple entry into the game is the giant play button on the main menu of the game, a tool that is popular in apps.

Older kids will tolerate a bit more ambiguity, but only if they're sufficiently motivated to play with the game. For example, if the game features their favorite character, they will sit for a longer time. But in general, there are just so many things competing for children's attention that a majority of kids are far more likely to put down the activity or game if they encounter a problem early on.

Instead, design for quick success and ease them into the more challenging parts.

Figure 16.2 A giant play button is easy for kids of all ages to understand and provides quick entry into the game as well as a feeling of accomplishment.

Toca Pet Doctor image used with permission of Toca Boca AB.

Create Games That Have Multiple Paths to a Correct Answer

Most of us have played *Math Blaster* or another game that was largely based on a quiz format and that rewarded you for quickly answering questions. But over the years, design and education have evolved to include many other styles of interaction.

There's an ongoing emphasis on helping grow children's interest in STEM—the fields of science, technology, engineering, and math—and games are a natural match. Not only do games present opportunities to explore all kinds of natural phenomena, such as the water cycle, genetics, and photosynthesis, but they also are the perfect opportunity to foster and grow a STEM mindset, not just the rote memorization of facts.

What does that mean?

The scientific process is about curiosity and discovery, as well as a process of hypothesis formation and testing. STEM education is also about inspiring in children the desire to find out on their own, not always simply to be taught. Games are a perfect opportunity to encourage kids to explore their environment, ask questions, and follow that curiosity beyond initial comprehension.

In our everyday lives, rarely is there just one way to solve the problem. While one solution may emerge as the most efficient (e.g., *Angry Birds* rewards us when we get the pigs with the fewest birds possible), life is not so black and white as to always require a single correct path.

Scribblenauts is perhaps my favorite game for practicing trial and error as well as for finding multiple solutions, because it moves away from a process-oriented pedagogy. Instead of always creating right and wrong answers, it encourages players to find different pathways to solve a problem. Each puzzle in the game has at least three solutions, and the player is rewarded for finding multiple solutions. For example, in the iOS game *Scribblenauts Remix*, one level asks the player to provide two things that a baker, firefighter, and policeman would use with their hands. Because the game is designed for multiple right answers, the baker could be given a rolling pin, bowl, knife, flour, or any of a number of other options.

Solving problems through trial and error is actually a really good strategy and not a waste of time. We often forget that wrong answers are a legitimate part of the innovation process. Wrong answers often lead to thoughts or information that eventually lead to a right answer. Games have the opportunity to foster a trial-and-error mindset in a key way; failure is encouraged, showing mistakes for what they are—part of the experimental process of finding an innovative solution.

Use Iconic, Consistent Design

When creating interfaces and defining functionality in kids' games, you will naturally want your interface to have a unique style and feel. While creating that style, remember to keep basic functionality and icons familiar and consistent with best practices. The basic interaction design is not a time to reinvent the wheel.

One of the easiest ways to think about this is to consider traffic signals—green means *go* and red means *stop* all around the world. The signage changes from place to place, but the basic message remains the same. It's the same in user interface design. A back arrow is an arrow pointing to the left. An X in a circle is used to indicate how to close an area. Green buttons mean *go* or *yes*. Red buttons mean *stop* or *no*.

If you're unsure what your target audience expects for icon design, you might ask some kids to draw the various buttons for you. Or look at competing products that are designed for the same audience.

Create Large Hot Spots

Whether you are developing for interaction via a touchscreen or a computer mouse, the hot spots have to be very large. Remember, too, that the younger the child, the larger the hot spot will need to be. Exactly how large depends on the size of your interface (e.g., iPhone versus iPad). User testing will help you confirm if your buttons are large enough. It also helps to look at successful products to see what others do.

If you have more than one hot spot on the screen, leave plenty of space between them so that kids don't touch the wrong one accidentally.

Avoid Long, Continuous Movements

A common interaction in kids' games requires the player to drag an item to a target location or to trace a pattern. With time and practice, kids improve in their ability to complete these actions accurately and without taking a break.

When dragging an object across the screen, however, most kids need to stop and look at their progress and make sure they're still headed in the right direction. Or their hand may be fatigued and need a moment of rest. When possible, avoid requiring a single continuous movement, and instead allow the child to complete the action in multiple steps.

This may mean allowing the child to trace a letter in stages. Or if the child is supposed to drag an item across the screen, do not snap the item back to the original location if it's dropped outside the target area; leave it instead at the furthest point of progress and let the child proceed from there. The iOS app *Elmo Loves 123s* from Sesame Workshop is a great example of an interaction that allows kids to trace numbers in stages, which is more forgiving for developing motor skills than requiring one continuous movement.

As with almost any guideline, there are exceptions to this. *LetterSchool* is a mobile app that helps kids learn to write letters. The game requires the player to trace letters in single, continuous actions. But the game is well designed to limit frustration with hints and scaffolds (discussed in chapter 19). So if the game design dictates that the player must make long, continuous actions, make sure the design also mitigates frustration.

Provide Visual Cues That Encourage Scrolling

While it seems that kids innately understand technology, not everything comes to them naturally. Scrolling, or understanding that there's more beyond what's visible on the screen, is a learned behavior.

When viewing websites or playing scrolling games, adults implicitly understand that there is more content than what is seen on the screen at any one time. We've learned through prior experience that these things have more content. We've also seen cues, such as scroll bars, and automatically understand what they mean.

Kids have to learn that there is more beyond the edges of the screen. Depending on their familiarity with technology, they may be seven or older before they understand scrolling on a regular basis. So when they visit a website, they do not automatically know to scroll down. Many preschool-targeted websites, including pbskids.org, create the most important content to be "above the fold," or visible without scrolling.

When you have more content than will fit on the screen, keep this in mind and design accordingly. First confirm that the design absolutely requires more content than will fit on the screen. Scrolling should not be implemented just because the designer is not being a good editor and reviewer of his own work. If scrolling is needed, then one option is to implement hierarchical menus rather than scrolling, so that making a selection on the main menu loads a new page with the submenu. But limit the number of layers, particularly for the younger ages. One level of abstraction can still present a challenge.

If you stick with scrolling, design the navigation with large arrows that look like buttons to help the child understand that there is more content beyond the screen. It's also useful to show a partial object at the sides of the scrolling area to further indicate that there is more content beyond the edges.

Beyond developing an understanding of where to expect scrolling content, preschoolers are also still developing their working memory,

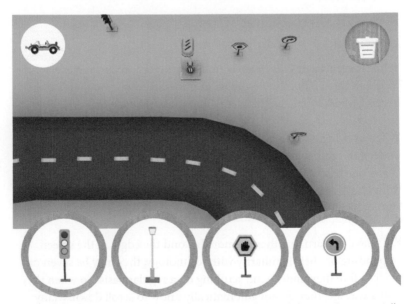

Figure 16.3 When using a scroll bar in your design, use visual clues, such as a partially visible object, to help kids realize that there is more content.

Toca Cars image used with permission of Toca Boca AB.

which can have a major impact on game design. Many puzzle games rely on the player's working memory as part of the gameplay. For example, in *Angry Birds*, you first see the target area and then the game pans across the screen to show the birds. As a player, you need to keep the target area in mind while aiming the birds.

That's really tough for young kids to do. Now, in addition to realizing that there is more content beyond the edge of the screen, they also have to keep the puzzle in mind while they strategize how to play the game. Advanced stuff!

When designing gameplay for kids, remember that they're still developing their working memory. It's fine to push them to use it, but don't overload it by requiring them to manage too many tasks at once.

Use Vivid Production Techniques Judiciously

Kids generally search for meaning in a story or game experience, and the vivid elements will capture their attention. In other words, the foremost object, the brightest object, the funniest object, and so on will be the focus of their attention. Make sure that that object is also the thing you want them to pay the most attention to. Otherwise, you could be creating a serious distraction.

Reduce the Risk of Children Making Accidental In-App Purchases

In-app purchases are common in mobile games, including children's apps featuring well-known brands such as *Highlights Hidden Pictures* or *Elmo Calls*. It's often referred to as the freemium model of game design—get the base app for free (or dirt cheap), then buy expansion packs and add-ons for cost within the app.

Most people have also heard the stories of thousands of dollars charged to accounts when kids make in-app purchases without realizing they are spending real money. While in-app purchases are often a necessary part of the business model, developers do have to implement the purchase features responsibly.

Apple and other publishing platforms increasingly have guidelines or requirements for how to do this, so, before you design the purchases in the game, check to see whether there are best practices already in place. But generally, the requirements are to put the purchases behind a gate that is difficult for children to access but appropriate for an adult. This, of course, varies depending on the target age.

For younger children, a gate that requires an advanced motor skill is often enough to stop them from accessing adult-oriented areas. For example, *ABC Wildlife* asks parents to swipe on the screen in a way that is difficult for children to do. For older children, developers often use a math problem or other word-based question is common.

Developers might also choose to provide reminders or a disclaimer noting that the purchase costs real money or to require an additional layer of confirmation before completing the purchase. Some developers also proactively provide additional information to parents on how to turn off in-app purchases completely.

Figure 16.4 Developers are encouraged to use methods to stop children from entering areas that are designed for adults with gesture gates, as in *ABC Wildlife*, or math problems that are difficult for children to answer.

ABC Wildlife image used with permission of Peapod Labs LLC.

Figure 16.5 Developers are increasingly including reminders that in-app purchases cost real money. This reminder is from the mobile game *Lost Light*.

Lost Light image used with permission of the Walt Disney Company.

Keep File Size to a Minimum for Downloadables

When reviewing a large number of apps over a short time period as part of a judging panel, I found myself installing a group of apps on my iPad and iPhone, reviewing them, and then deleting them in order to make room for the next group of apps. The file sizes were varied, but, man, did I come to feel affectionate toward the smaller ones. And it got me thinking that if I'm going through this install-delete-install-delete rigmarole because I really *have* to review these apps, how does an average parent feel when confronted with this situation?

Take a minute and think about a busy mom, who is installing her latest and greatest app finds on her iPad for Junior. But, alas, there's no room for the super-mega, enormous App of Awesome, which tips the scales at 785 megabytes! If she's smart, this parent has already turned off the delete functionality, probably after her child accidentally erased her Gmail, *New York Times*, and Facebook apps for the third time. So now, if she wants to install App of Awesome, Mom has to change that setting, delete the other apps, photos, music, or movies that she can live without (once she's figured out what those are), and then go and re-install the app.

The odds are incredibly slim that any large app from an unknown company is going to get past all of these hurdles.

There may be justifications in some cases for having a larger app, like a lot of embedded video or a complex game experience, but for a consumer it has to feel worthwhile. Companies like Nickelodeon can get away with larger file sizes because people know they're likely to get something of good quality. If you're an unknown, customers may well give up on your app rather than make the effort to install it.

Good development practices mean that there are things you can do to minimize file size, and your programmer should be on top of this (but may need a reminder). Some points to consider are these:
- Make sure unnecessary code bits and files that were used in development are not bundled in the final app.
- Optimize image sizes for your device.
- When writing your voiceover script, remember that voiceover is a huge source of file bloat. Often, you can word things more simply and use repeated phrases rather than wording something slightly differently. A really good audio editor can also help you design ways to maximize efficiency.

- Most of all, let your programmer know that file size is a concern from the get-go so that he or she can keep it in mind—after all, why should the programmer worry about file size unless it's an issue for you?

In the end, there is no optimal size or final guideline. The size of a product will change as the amount of storage improves on devices. So the file size truly depends on what you need for the experience and what you can justify to your audience.

CHAPTER 17
Considerations for Interactions by Platform or Device

Many aspects of good design are universal, but, depending on the device or platform that will host your game, there are affordances and features to consider.

This chapter explores considerations related to a number of gaming platforms, including desktop Web interfaces, touchscreens (including smartphones and tablets), motion-based controls, and, to a limited extent, video game console platforms. We offer points to consider for the following platforms and devices:

- Computer mouse and trackpad interactions
- Touchscreens
- Stylus-based interactions
- Gaming controllers
- Motion-based controls
- Camera interactions
- Microphone interactions

Computer Mouse or Trackpad-Based Interactions

Though it sometimes seems we're living in an entirely mobile world, kids still play many games on desktop computers, using a computer mouse or trackpad. The games may be hosted on websites and include stand-alone games, like those on PBS Kids or Nickelodeon, and virtual worlds, like *Club Penguin* or *Moshi Monsters*; games may also be downloadable and played via Steam or as a software application on the computer. Kids also are likely to use computer interfaces at school as well.

The following are considerations specific to designing an interaction employing a computer mouse or trackpad. In other words, these are games in which the player is controlling the game on a device that's not a touchable screen.

Using a device to interact with the screen is an abstract concept that requires precise fine motor skills, especially for younger children.

Using a computer mouse introduces a level of abstraction that is hard for younger children who are still learning cause and effect. They have to use one hand to move a device that's controlling something on a screen, often a few feet away.

Not only is it hard to understand that one thing in one hand is controlling something on the screen; it requires precise fine motor skills to use it accurately. So the younger the child, the more forgiving the interface must be, especially for mouse-based interactions. Keyboards, particularly arrow keys, may help make it easier for kids to play the games.

Drag-and-drop interactions are really tough for developing motor skills.

A lot of games include moving objects from one place to another. It's a common interaction mechanic. The most common design options include:
- Click-to-select, where the user clicks on the object of interest and it automatically jumps to the target location.
- Drag-and-drop, where the user has to maintain a button press while moving the object to the target location. This often includes multiple

steps—the user selects the object by pressing down on the mouse, maintains the button press while moving it to the target location, and then releases the button while keeping the object located over the target location.

- Click-and-carry, where the user can click on the object to automatically attach the item to the cursor location until the mouse is clicked again. There are generally four steps: move the cursor to the object; press and release the mouse button; move the cursor to the target location; press and release the mouse button again.

Not surprisingly, click-to-select is the easiest, and click-and-carry is much easier than drag-and-drop. Drag-and-drop challenges kids' hotspot targeting skills, and we know these are inaccurate and unpredictable at best for preschoolers and dependent on the child's fine motor skills as they get older. Furthermore, they need to maintain constant pressure on the mouse button, which is hard enough for developing muscles, and they need to move the mouse to the final location while maintaining the pressure. That's asking a lot of their developing motor skills, whereas click-and-carry allows more room for error and is easier for kids.

If you have to use a drag-and-drop style of interaction, remember that kids' motor skills are developing. Don't punish the player for an inability to drag the object all the way to the final spot in a single try by snapping the object back to the origination point.

Instead, allow the user to move the object incrementally across the screen. If the child picks up the object and drags it halfway before releasing, let the object stay in that spot. Then the child can pick it up and move it further.

At times, the gameplay may not allow for this incremental movement. When that's the case, level the game design accordingly. Easier levels might move the objects shorter distances to allow the child to practice these developing motor skills.

Touchscreens

Touchscreen-based technology, such as smartphones and tablets as well as, increasingly, larger screens, is a dominant part of children's lives. It often seems that kids naturally know how to interact with a screen that they can touch. Cognitively, it makes sense. Where a computer mouse requires a level of understanding of cause and effect to make things happen on a screen that is a distance away, the touchscreen simply requires touching the thing that you want to interact with. It's direct mapping instead of abstraction.

But designing for touchscreens is not without challenges when it comes to children. Here are guidelines for touchscreen interactions. Several points also apply when the player is asked to use a stylus to interact with the game, as with a Nintendo 3DS.

It's common for the player to obscure part of the screen with her hand.

As a child (or an adult) interacts with a touchscreen, part of the hand and arm may obscure the screen, particularly on tablets. While adults generally use short-term memory to visualize the screen, children may not yet be practiced at this, particularly if they have to keep multiple pieces of information in mind at the same time.

The child is most likely to obscure part of the screen when the task is to move something around the screen or to trace an objects; the hand obscures part of the path or target area, so the child lifts his hand to check where he's going.

It's unavoidable that the player will obscure the screen, particularly because, as a developer, you cannot guarantee that your user will always use the right or left hand to interact with the game. In other words, you can't design your game to always be played by a right-handed person and place the nonessential information in areas that would be obscured by the player's right arm!

On average, kids do not settle into a hand preference (e.g., right-handed or left-handed) until they are around age 6. Even once they settle on a hand, they are still likely to switch hands while interacting with touchscreens, especially on simpler tasks involving tapping or moving objects around the screen.

As with the guideline suggesting that you avoid penalizing the player who is struggling to move an object across the screen, keep in mind

Figure 17.1 Kids may sometimes accidentally touch a screen with two or three fingers simultaneously or touch the screen with the hand that's holding the device.

Image used under Creative Commons Attribution License from Flickr member Jenny Downing.

when designing touchscreen interactions that the player may from time to time have to lift his arm to see the entire screen. Avoid snapping the object back to the starting position or requiring that the child start over whenever possible.

Plan for accidental touches.

Kids are notorious for wandering fingers that accidentally touch the screen, making the app not respond because the code interprets the wandering finger as the intended touch. They also might touch with two or three fingers at the same time or accidentally touch the screen with the hand that is holding the device.

While almost anyone new to touchscreen technologies will do this (including grandparents!), kids take longer to learn to be aware of their body. So an adult will quickly learn to hold the device differently. Kids, on the other hand, may become frustrated and think the game is broken.

Depending on how much trouble this could cause their product, developers tackle this issue in a variety of ways. Some add a safe zone around the edges of the screen, since the edges are most vulnerable to accidental touches while holding the device. Others develop schemas for throwing out touches if they're held for too long. The method for handling the touches really depends on the product, but it's worth looking into if your user testing indicates that extraneous touches pose a risk.

If the interface doesn't have room for a safe-zone border around the edges (if you're developing for a smartphone interface, for example), then remember that the upper corners seem to be accidentally touched less than the bottom area.

Make something noticeable and/or audible happen on touch.

When navigating with a computer mouse, it's standard to implement onPress and rollover states for buttons and clickable elements. This confirms that the click has been registered. On touchscreens, it's harder to see the onPress state when it's hidden under the finger. Kids, who are not as accurate with their touches because their motor skills are still developing, need feedback that their touch was registered when they touch the screen. They don't intuitively lift their finger from the screen to see if the touch was registered.

Building in an audible sound when the object is pressed helps. Also effective is a visual change that is larger than the fingerprint, such as a circle appearing around the object or a shift of the object.

Also related to this idea is that kids seem to expect something to happen when they touch the screen (onPress), rather than when they lift their finger from the screen (onLift). This is contrary to mouse-based interactions on the computer, where we are used to events happening when the mouse button is released. As an extreme example of this, I've

Figure 17.2 In *Sago Mini Sound Box*, a circle appears around the object when it is pressed. This helps the child know that her touch has been registered by the software since she may not be able to see the target under her finger.

Sago Mini Sound Box image used with permission of Sago Sago.

seen kids touch a screen and wait for a response without lifting their finger. When the software did not respond, rather than lift their finger from the screen, the kids pressed harder on the screen!

Focus on input gestures that are developmentally appropriate.

Just as kids must learn to scroll down a screen, they also must learn to use gestures like pinching and pulling apart (e.g., for zooming in and out), which require multifinger coordination and a wide finger span. These fine motor gestures present additional challenges for kids as they are still learning to coordinate the movements of their fingers.

The size of the gesture relative to a child's hand should also be considered. For example, if the task requires the child to stretch a box until it fills a large part of the screen, the child may need to use two hands, whereas an adult might use one hand. The child's finger span is much smaller than an adult's and should be considered in tandem with the complexity of the gesture.

Stylus

Developmentally, using a stylus to interact with a touchscreen device is very similar to holding a pencil or other writing tool. A child's writing grip develops until a child is around 10 or 11 years old. The ability to hold a pencil with a mature grip, which is what most adults are used to, also depends on how much coaching the child receives to shift to the mature grip.

The evolution of the grip changes throughout childhood. At young ages, children grip the pencil with their entire fist. The grip can also depend on the task—a child may switch to a less mature grip when coloring in large areas but use a more mature or normal grip when writing letters or making other fine motor skill movements.

Because children use a variety of grips to hold the stylus, they may make contact with the screen at unusual angles. Depending on the hardware, this may mean that the child's input will not be recognized at all. Or if the child is dragging an object across the screen but using the stylus at an odd angle, the software might think the child has released the object. As with other input mechanisms, be careful that your game does not overly penalize children who are still developing these fine motor skills.

Figure 17.3 When using a stylus or any writing tool, kids will hold it in many ways.

Image used under Creative Commons Attribution License from Flickr member Claudia Rahanmetan.

Gaming Controllers

Like other button-based interaction devices, gaming controllers are easier to work as the child ages. Controllers such as those for the Xbox or PlayStation are particularly complicated because of the number of buttons and the size of the controller. Perhaps it's easiest to think of the optimal number of buttons as being correlated with age. The older the child, the more buttons she should be able to manage.

Developing games specifically for children to play on the gaming consoles is uncommon in today's market. The kids who do tend to play are generally playing games that were designed for a larger general audience. Or, if you are lucky enough to be developing a children's console game, it is likely focused on peripherals, such as a dance mat or motion-based controls, that do not require children to use the buttons as a significant part of gameplay. Physical interactions are discussed later in this chapter.

Figure 17.4 Gaming consoles are enticing to kids but present challenges related to the size of the controller as well as the number of buttons.

Image used under Creative Commons Attribution License by Flickr member makelessnoise.

Motion-Based Controls

Kids are incredibly physical and constantly in motion. A number of platforms allow games to take advantage of this physical energy. The Xbox Kinect uses cameras to do motion tracking. Accelerometers and gyroscopes in smartphones and tablets allow the child to tip the device to control objects on screen.

With these controls come a number of considerations, centered around gross motor skills. In general, as the child ages, his skill at physical inputs will increase as well. Just as kids are developing fine motor skills, they are also refining through practice their gross motor skills, the large motions such as jumping, walking, or throwing a ball. They are also practicing their ability to balance and increasing their ability to endure longer periods of physicality. Even walking requires the ability to balance on one leg while shifting weight to the other leg; children become steady with this form of balance around age 5 or 6. They are also developing coordination and awareness of their body.

Be forgiving for gestural controls.

Remember that preschoolers are often still learning skills and are likely to be inaccurate in their gestures. If your game will involve the use of gestural controls or motion-based game mechanics, be forgiving and err on the side of positive feedback. Kids fidget a lot, too, which causes a lot of noise in the data.

As an example of the wide range of abilities among children, watch preschoolers jump. Some will tell you they jumped when they barely got off the ground. Others will get quite far off the ground. Your games will be played by kids with all ranges of ability.

Kids are constantly in motion, so the data will be noisy.

If you ask a child to stand still, she will likely still fidget (though you can hope she'll stay in one place). When the main game input is motion based, kids' natural inclination to shift around will cause a lot of noise in the data. This can make it very difficult to discern one type of motion from another in a relatively quick fashion. As sensors improve, the ability of software to make quick decisions will improve.

Build in breaks for active interfaces.

Preschoolers are not good at taking breaks when they're tired. They haven't yet learned to recognize the signs their body is sending. Parents and caregivers often intervene and establish break times for kids. But, as a developer, you can also identify logical moments for breaks and encourage them within the game. Limit round lengths to a reasonable amount of time.

In some games, build in explicit break times to allow the player to rest, which also reinforces healthy habits. For example, a minigame in *Sesame Street: Ready, Set, Grover* on the Nintendo Wii allows the child to jump up to 100 times with Elmo. Every 20 jumps, the game pauses and Elmo takes a drink of water. Sesame Street also does this with the iOS app *Rosita's Jump Counts*. During the kid testing of the app, they found that kids would jump endlessly and exhaust themselves.

Limit the length of time the player has to stay in a position.

When designing actions or poses that you want the player to use, keep in mind that some poses are easier to hold than others. For example, it's difficult to hold your arm in the air in front of you for a long period of time. But using your arm to gesture through menus is a common control for the Kinect. If the child is navigating the menus, she may need time to rest her arm.

Harder actions limit body movement more than easy actions.

If the goal of the game is to get people moving, then easier actions, such as flapping arms or jumping, will encourage more movement. The harder the movements, the more the player has to concentrate, which means he will move with more hesitation.

Dance games are great for seeing this effect. Players jump all over on easy levels but tend to restrict their movements once they start playing harder levels.

Kids don't stay where they're supposed to.

If the child is standing and playing a game, he will move around the room. This presents a safety concern, as he has reduced awareness of his

Figure 17.5 Kids inevitably move toward the television when playing games or watching videos, which can present safety concerns as well as compromise the gaming experience.

Image used under Creative Commons Attribution License by Flickr member Peter Dutton.

surroundings. It also presents a hardware performance concern if the game is being played on a television and gaming console. For example, if the child is playing an Xbox Kinect game, the child will inevitably move toward the television while playing. But in order for the Kinect sensors to work properly, the child must be at least six feet from the sensors. Developers therefore have to design reminders into the game to tell the child to move to an appropriate position.

Cameras

The proliferation of smartphones and tablets means that developers working on those platforms can integrate cameras and photos into their games and activities. For young children, seeing themselves or familiar friends and family in the game is a delight that makes the experience intensely personal. Older kids are also exploring their social identity, so the ability to use images to personalize the experience and interact with the game appeals to their sense of ego formation. Interactive tools like StoryBots allow the player to personalize stories and games in just this way.

Player-created images can also provide additional gameplay, such as using the camera to take a photo of a color or a texture for a coloring activity. Or they can be used in augmented-reality apps, where the software scans the image for particular shapes. *Big Bird's Words* is a mobile app that makes a game of finding words in print. In this vocabulary-building game from Sesame Street, the player is prompted to find particular words and then use the camera to scan the word.

Young children need help aiming the camera.

Kids are not born knowing how to take selfies. They have to learn to aim the camera and take photos. Not to mention that it can be hard to hold the device steady and press the button to take the photo. So, when incorporating the camera into a game, make sure you support the child (or the parent).

Sometimes it might even be possible to simply show the camera feed in the game, such as in the *Pat the Bunny* app. In this e-book, the camera allows the child to see his reflection in the mirror.

Photos can contain personal information.

If you're planning to allow the child to share the photo, either in the game or through e-mail tools built into the device, be sure you confirm with a qualified professional that you're within the privacy laws. Photos can be automatically tagged with information that could be considered personal and is therefore subject to privacy laws in certain countries.

Microphones

Kids have great access to microphones as well as cameras in today's devices. It's long been known that kids will talk back to television. Watch *Dora the Explorer* with a preschooler to see this in action. Microphones mean that the software can ask for the child's input and interact with her or serve as a tool for documenting her stories.

Some of my favorite videos of preschoolers playing games show preschoolers singing along in *Rock Band* or other karaoke games.

Figure 17.6 In *Sago Mini Doodlecast*, the child draws a picture. While he's drawing, the software can record the child's narration, which creates an archive of the drawing. Some kids use the software to tell a story or send messages as part of their picture.

Sago Mini Doodlecast image used with permission of Sago Sago.

They're able to master surprisingly complex songs, and it makes for a great opportunity for families to play together.

But when karaoke games are bigger than your budget can handle, any simple interactions with the microphone are great for preschoolers. I say "simple interactions" because a number of projects have attempted speech recognition with preschoolers. Thus far, it's proven too difficult to do accurately. Preschoolers are often hard to understand, especially when they're learning new words, which makes it next to impossible for speech recognition algorithms to work effectively.

Simple interactions often take the form of what you see on preschool television. A character will ask a question and wait for an answer. During that waiting time, the developer has an equalizer on the screen that bounces with any sound the microphone "hears." It creates a simple effect of the game or character interacting with the child. The Disney Junior Appisode *Road Rally* uses this interaction.

AutoRap by Smule is a mobile app that allows you to record yourself talking, perhaps saying a poem. It then autotunes your spoken words and plays them over a rap beat. While the app is not designed for children, I've seen many kids, including preschoolers, spend huge chunks of time playing with it.

Similarly, apps such as *Talking Tom* allow you to record a small snippet of sound and hear it repeated back by the character, often in a slightly garbled tone. Many have chosen to use the garbled tone to help avoid the situation where a character is then saying something inappropriate for children, like curse words. But allowing the child to record her voice and hear it played back remains a really interesting and engaging play pattern.

Deploying on Multiple Platforms

It's often a necessity to publish games on multiple device sizes, such as iPad and iPhone. If you're an Android developer, you might also release a game on multiple devices of widely varying sizes. It's also not uncommon to release a desktop version controlled with a keyboard or mouse as well as iOS and Android versions.

One UI does not fit all.

When designing for multiple screen sizes, consider how the experience will feel on each device. Some developers prefer to start with the smallest device and then size up. Others work from the largest. Regardless, these designers think through the user experience on all different sizes.

Viewing the PBS KIDS website on iPad and iPhone presents very different experiences. Similarly, the *New York Times* has very different experiences depending on which device you use to view the content.

The more you can test your game with your target audience on the various platforms, the better you'll understand how users will interact with the game on that particular device. You may find that some games are not a fulfilling experience on one device. For example, when we made the multitouch puzzle game *Williamspurrrrg*, it was clear that it would never work on the iPhone—touching the screen with ten fingers at once while still leaving space to look at the screen is impossible!

Similarly, the different experiences users have with smartphones and tablets are not limited to interface decisions. Some developers implement a shake mechanic on smaller devices but do not use it for tablets, mostly for fear that the child will drop the larger, more cumbersome device.

CHAPTER 18
Making Educational and Commercial Games

Is your product educational? Is it commercial? Is it for the home market or for schools? As much as most developers would like to say yes to every market possible, most games for kids need to focus on a primary market first.

The question whether a game is educational or commercial can be difficult to answer. In part, it depends on the target age. A game for preschoolers is likely both educational and commercial because children in that age group don't have an aversion to anything labeled educational!

This chapter explores:
- What it means to be educational
- Selecting an educational topic
- Using educational standards
- Working with educational advisors
- Developing games for in-school use

What Does It Mean to Be Educational?

If a product specifically says it is educational, it means it is designed with a specific learning goal in mind. For example, it might teach letter sounds, math facts, or American history. The idea is that after playing with the product, the child will have had exposure to a concept and an opportunity to practice the concept. She may not have mastered it or be able to transfer it to another setting, but the intent is to support her learning.

Educational games may teach hard skills, such as math facts, or softer skills, such as understanding emotions. Or they may be aligned with curriculum standards that are used by schools.

If you decide that it is valuable to align with curriculum standards, you should have someone with the appropriate credentials decide how and whether the game aligns with standards. While you can easily declare that your product aligns with a particular standard, curriculum standards can be slippery and confusing, so it's best to have a teacher or educational consultant review your product to make sure that it is, indeed, aligned with the standard.

A commercial product has a primary goal of entertaining the player. It does not necessarily forgo being educational, but that goal definitely takes a back seat. Many commercial games that were designed for entertainment purposes end up being educational. It's the nature of games to go hand in hand with certain skills, such as problem solving and engineering. *Minecraft*, in which players build worlds from 3D blocks, is often used in schools to teach a number of subjects as well as to encourage kids to learn about 3D engineering. *Portal*, a puzzle game in which players have to solve problems by thinking three-dimensionally, is used to help kids practice problem solving and flexible thinking. *Dance Dance Revolution*, a physically active game in which players dance on a mat in time to the music, has been researched in numerous settings and has been shown to help players lose weight and make friends.

Selecting an Educational Topic

Sometimes the educational topic is part of the game's mandate. For example, you might receive a request to pitch an educational game for iPad that's focused on emotions. Other times, you may be free to choose whatever you want. How do you go about picking an educational topic?

First, become familiar with the educational goals of the age group you're targeting. You may find that one set of educational goals stands out as interesting to you. At the same time, play as many games for the target age group as you can. Are there topics that are covered repeatedly, such as the ABCs and 123s? Are there gaps in the market that you believe you can address? You might also talk to parents, teachers, and kids and find out what they're looking for or what they think is missing.

If a developer focuses on one of the common and heavily used topics, she runs the risk of being thoroughly overshadowed by the big brands. For example, almost every one of the preschool properties for Disney, Nick Jr., and PBS KIDS has covered the ABCs. I'd say that most of the book publishers have covered the subject as well. If you're launching a new, unknown IP or are a small or independent studio, how can you expect to compete with that? There are so many great and needed topics to cover that are far more than another concept focused on "A is for . . ."

That said, as much as I think it's better to identify and address gaps in the market, a lot of developers find themselves faced with figuring out how to put a fresh face on an already heavily competitive topic, such as the ABCs. It's certainly happened to me! I strongly suggest developers who are executing ideas on common themes do everything they can to stand out.

For example, memory games are among the most common games for kids, especially preschoolers. Yes, they're simple to program. But there are so many other game mechanics that can be used for preschoolers. I was perfectly happy to never see another memory game until I saw *Memory Match: Starring You!* from Storybots. While it is a memory game, the images can be personalized with photos of friends and family, so the developers modified the game for today's technology and audience.

If you have to do a game mechanic or concept that has already been done hundreds of times before, take the time to differentiate your product. It'll help your product stand out in the sea of competition.

Educational Standards

Schools use curriculum standards to help codify and standardize what kids learn across numerous topics, including English language arts, mathematics, and sciences. In the United States, the Common Core State Standards Initiative is one way to maintain consistency across a large geographic area. The U.S. Common Core standards cover English language arts and mathematics for kindergarten to grade 12.

These are Common Core standards for kindergarten English language arts, specific to literature.

CCSS.ELA-LITERACY.RL.K.1
With prompting and support, ask and answer questions about key details in a text.

CCSS.ELA-LITERACY.RL.K.5
Recognize common types of texts (e.g., storybooks, poems).

CCSS.ELA-LITERACY.RL.K.9
With prompting and support, compare and contrast the adventures and experiences of characters in familiar stories.

These are Common Core standards for grades 11–12 English language arts, specific to literature.

CCSS.ELA-LITERACY.RL.11–12.1
Cite strong and thorough textual evidence to support analysis of what the text says explicitly as well as inferences drawn from the text, including determining where the text leaves matters uncertain.

CCSS.ELA-LITERACY.RL.11–12.5
Analyze how an author's choices concerning how to structure specific parts of a text (e.g., the choice of where to begin or end a story, the choice to provide a comedic or tragic resolution) contribute to its overall structure and meaning as well as its aesthetic impact.

CCSS.ELA-LITERACY.R.L.11–12.9
Demonstrate knowledge of eighteenth-, nineteenth- and early-twentieth-century foundational works of American literature,

including how two or more texts from the same period treat similar themes or topics.

These are Common Core standards for kindergarten mathematics, specific to geometry.

CCSS.MATH.CONTENT.K.G.A.1
Describe objects in the environment using names of shapes, and describe the relative positions of these objects using terms such as *above, below, beside, in front of, behind*, and *next to*.

CCSS.MATH.CONTENT.K.G.B.5
Model shapes in the world by building shapes from components (e.g., sticks and clay balls) and drawing shapes.

These are Common Core standards for grade 8 mathematics, specific to geometry.

CCSS.MATH.CONTENT.8.G.A.4
Understand that a two-dimensional figure is similar to another if the second can be obtained from the first by a sequence of rotations, reflections, translations, and dilations; given two similar two-dimensional figures, describe a sequence that exhibits the similarity between them.

CCSS.MATH.CONTENT.8.G.C.9
Know the formulas for the volumes of cones, cylinders, and spheres and use them to solve real-world and mathematical problems.

The Common Core Standards are often broad and subject to interpretation, so they do not represent a perfect system. However, curriculum standards provide an excellent reference for developers on what skills should be targeted for an age group. Developers often spell out which of the Common Core standards their product is aligned with. For example, the website for *Slice Fractions* from Ululab lists the standards its products meet.

Whether your product needs to specifically call out Common Core standards depends on the specific educational goals. If you plan to align your product with standards of any type, it's best to work with someone familiar with the interpretation and use of the standards in the classroom, such as a teacher.

Working with Educational Advisers

With educational goals often comes the need to work with educational advisers. I've been in both roles, as a developer who seeks the approval of the educational adviser and also as the educational adviser who is looking out for the child's best interest.

One Adviser Does Not Fit All

One of the greatest challenges in choosing educational advisers is finding one who fits with the philosophy of the team, intellectual property, or company. Sometimes the educational adviser is part of the brand development, which simplifies matters. But if you have to find an adviser, first identify candidates by asking colleagues, checking the credits of similar titles to see who advised the developers, or searching the table of contents of educational journals or lists of speakers at academic conferences. Teachers often make great educational advisers, too.

Generally, you want a subject matter expert, someone who understands the educational curriculum deeply. At the same time, you want someone who is flexible enough to work within entertainment. Tension frequently arises when the educational adviser says the best practice is to implement a skill in a particular way but the recommended way is the least fun and interesting from a game design perspective. The hope is that your adviser will work with you to navigate the educational curriculum and best practices in a way that is enjoyable and beneficial to the child. Both sides will have to compromise.

It's an added benefit if your adviser has worked on previous games, as he'll be familiar with the production schedule and the way the game develops. If he is new to the process, let him know what to expect, including bugs, placeholder art, and scratch audio, so he won't get frustrated or be surprised.

When to Bring in Advisers

While no two projects are exactly the same, this is a fairly common advisory schedule.

- Kick-off: Bring the adviser(s) and team together. Let the advisers discuss the best practices of the educational goals. Then brainstorm as a team.
- Design review: At the point that you have paper designs, send them to the advisory board to review. Sometimes this step is positioned as an update to let the board know what came out of the kick-off meeting.
- Final asset review: When you're getting close to finalizing assets such as script art or anything else that has a significant impact on the educational goals, send them to the relevant advisers.
- Alpha review: Either meet the adviser in person to walk him through the game or talk with him by phone before and after he reviews the game to discuss his feedback. This step may be repeated with several playable prototypes, depending on how your team develops.
- Beta review: This is usually more of a courtesy than a specific point for feedback.

I usually add extra hours to the adviser's contract, sometimes as much as an hour a week, for questions that inevitably pop up. I might want a quick gut check on an interface or idea, or I might want him to review the user testing protocol.

If you plan to use the adviser's credentials as part of your game marketing, make sure you clear that with the adviser. Depending on the adviser's institution, there may be restrictions on what he can endorse publicly.

Developing Games to Be Played in Schools

Perhaps you've heard complaints about the state of school technology? That schools are full of old machines, broken smart boards, outdated software, and policies that won't allow installation of new programs? While some schools have shiny new tablets, many schools truly are that bad. Most grants that are written for in-school research have to include line items for hardware, software, and technical support.

For developers, this often means developing to a far lower common denominator than is ideal, which can be incredibly frustrating. The management/sales teams may have to maintain a strong relationship with the schools to ensure that the school's technology can meet your minimal technical requirements.

A common mistake is to assume that the state of technology in a fancy private school today represents where the public schools will be three years from now. So it's simply a matter of lasting that long. Sadly, developers have been thinking that for decades. School systems just do not evolve that quickly, at least not without significant help.

So if you are developing for schools, the best thing you can do is make friends with as many teachers, principals, parents, and technology directors as possible, along with anyone else familiar with the school infrastructure. Test frequently with your target audience in the target locations to ensure that you are on track.

CHAPTER 19

Instructions, Tutorials, Scaffolding, and In-Game Help

In a perfect world, no game would require instructions. A child would simply pick it up and know intuitively how to play it. Unfortunately, we're not living in that perfect world!

Tutorials and instructions explain how to play the game and generally happen automatically in the first levels of the game (or the first play experience) and then are available for the player to reference as needed. Some games also add in-game hints and support to help the player throughout the gameplay experience.

The wide range of children's abilities also means that the game itself must be playable by users at many different skill levels. Usability can take many forms depending on the type of game you're making, but fundamentally it involves the idea of scaffolding, or in-game help systems to assist the player when they're stuck. Beyond good tutorials and instructions, scaffolding unfolds in many ways during gameplay.

Scaffolding, in the classic instructional design form, is what teachers and caregivers do quite naturally when interacting with learners. It generally involves a series of actions in which the teacher intervenes to:
- Grab the student's attention
- Create and adjust the task to moderate frustration
- Model and demonstrate the task where needed
- Provide encouragement and motivation
- Highlight task features that are most relevant to the learning goals and the student's abilities

When implementing scaffolding in games, you can accomplish all these goals to varying degrees. However, perhaps the greatest opportunity specific to games and scaffolding is the idea of real-time intervention. In the classroom, this is the idea that, rather than wait for a report card or test scores to evaluate the child's performance, educators continually assess the child's progress and make adjustments in real-time. It's also sometimes referred to as just-in-time intervention.

Games provide an opportunity to continually assess the player and make adjustments to the experience according to the needs of the individual. With that in mind, this chapter focuses on best practices for supporting your player throughout the game, including:

- Finding the balance between too much and too little support
- Assuming that the player has never played before
- Determining tutorial length
- Skipping tutorials
- Providing visual support
- Offering hints during gameplay
- Testing instructions
- Repeating instructions
- Allowing the player to adjust the game difficulty
- Automatically adjusting the game difficulty based on player performance
- Providing encouragement and motivation

Strive for Just Enough Support but Not Too Much, Which Is Easier Said Than Done

It's easy to find anecdotes of young children swiping, pinching, and zooming their way through touchscreen interfaces. "It's innate!" many of these anecdotes will cry. However, when you understand the developmental side of things, it remains that these are still learned behaviors, just like scrolling. But young children pick them up very quickly, so quickly that they often appear innate.

Because preschoolers are still learning these tools for interaction, you should design products for them as if you were developing the player's first experience with the technology. For many, it truly will be their first time as technology is not so ubiquitous. Support what they can do next with gentle highlights and clear UI design. Introduce additional features gradually over time, across levels. (Try playing *Plants vs Zombies* for a general-audience version of how to phase in and explain functionality over time.)

While you want to provide enough support for those who are brand new to the experience, the challenge is that the instructions must also get out of the way for those who are familiar with the game. Don't require lengthy tutorials or complicated gates at the beginning of the experience. This is another time when user testing is critical to helping you understand how much support is needed and how much is too much.

Assume That Your Player Has Never Played a Game Before

Even though most kids have played a game before, there will always be kids who are coming to games for the first time or, at a minimum, coming to your type of game for the first time. So you have to plan for the players who have never played before by including tutorials and support for people who aren't sure what to do.

Casual games, such as *Angry Birds* or *Cut the Rope*, have this challenge, too—many in their audience of players would never categorize themselves as gamers, yet they play these games that fill the little moments of downtime in our days. These folks are unlikely to have deep experience or familiarity with basic gaming conventions. As such, the design teams carefully develop the games so that inexperienced players feel empowered to continue (while at the same time making sure they don't bore the experienced gamers out of their minds).

Do Not Start with a Long Tutorial Video

Far too many games simply begin with an extended tutorial video on how to play the game, but children (like adults) have little patience for extended instructions/videos. While a short introduction can help to set the stage (and by short, I mean five seconds!), remember that kids have an expectation that they will be *playing* the game, not watching. Approach instructions as a need-to-know experience—tell them only what they need to know in order to play that moment in the game. Then insert additional tutorials at the relevant places as new rules or objects are introduced.

For example, in *Motion Math: Zoom*, the player first learns to place numbers along the number line. During the first minutes of gameplay, the number line has all numbers visible. But eventually, the number line collapses and only 10s are visible (10, 20, 30, and so on). In order to place numbers in between, such as 15, the player has to expand the number line by pulling apart the number line.

When this interaction is introduced, an animation is shown to help the player understand how to expand the number line. While this information is housed within a tutorial level, the player is given time

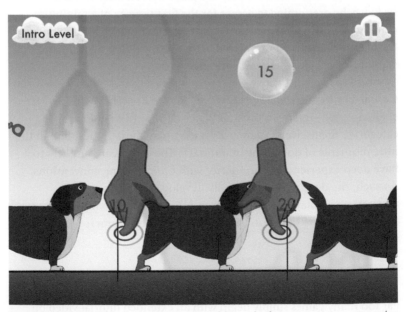

Figure 19.1 *Motion Math: Zoom* provides additional information as new gameplay tools are introduced. In this example, the animation helps guide the player through the pull-apart gesture.

Image used with permission of Motion Math Inc.

to master the first interaction—placing numbers on the number line—before learning the second interaction—expanding the number line. Rather than overload the player with all of the necessary rules of play, good tutorial design introduces the information as needed.

Allow Players to Skip Any Introductory Text or Tutorials

Just as your game will have new players, it will also have experienced players who simply want to skip the instructions. Give them an option that allows them to get into gameplay quickly. A skip button or X button is a commonly recognized icon.

Provide Simple, Visual Instructions

Whenever possible, avoid relying on audio or text to explain how to play the game. The volume may be turned off on the device or the child may not be able to read, so well-designed visual instructions will be key. If you've ever seen instructions for assembling Ikea furniture, then you've

Figure 19.2 *Motion Math: Zoom* provides simple visual instructions that can be understood without the ability to read.

Image used with permission of Motion Math Inc.

seen a great example of entirely visual instructions. Granted, they can be really long and complicated, but they communicate an extraordinary amount of information without words.

Provide Help at the Moments When the Player Is Stuck

A tutorial at the beginning of the game (or when new mechanics are introduced) is great for teaching initial gameplay. But players also need help when they get stuck during the game. This help can take many forms.

Usability support, such as guiding the player's attention to a particular button or area of the screen, is often done without interrupting gameplay via a visual highlight or pop-up. Pop-ups can also be used to let the player know that more help is available.

If the player appears stuck in *Motion Math: Zoom*, the game pops up a message that says, "Want help? Yes" that the player can tap on. The game then automatically scrolls to the correct answer. The player can then answer the question. But the game then resets to the moment where the player asked for help and repeats the question, so the player does not get a free pass to skip the question. He still has to answer it.

The original *Motion Math* game, which focuses on fractions, has a great initial tutorial, where the player must first master the mechanic of tilting the device to control the falling ball. But I am particularly fond of the way the developers scaffold the player if she is struggling to find the correct answer.

In the game, the player must tilt the device side to side in order to place a fraction on a number line. If the player is not answering correctly, the game presents a variety of visual supports to guide the player to the correct answer. The images of a sample problem, where the player must place the fraction 2/3 onto the number line, are shown here.

- In the first image, the player tries without scaffolding.
- After the first error, an arrow points in the correct direction.
- After the second error, the number line is divided into segments relative to the fraction.

Figure 19.3

Figure 19.4

Figure 19.5

Figure 19.6

Figure 19.7

Motion Math provides a series of visual supports to guide players to the correct answer. (Figures 19.3 to 19.7.)

Images used with permission of Motion Math Inc.

- After the third error, the number line is labeled with the fractions. The correct answer is left blank, providing a visual cue of where the fraction belongs.
- After the fourth error, an arrow points to the correct answer.

Another children's game that provides thoughtful visual scaffolding is *LetterSchool*. The activity design is well leveled to increase in difficulty. Within the most difficult levels, the player is charged with tracing the letter with no visual cues, though the player is never without help if it is needed. The player is first presented the letter to be traced, such as the letter G. The letter fades, leaving just the key targets of the letter. Then only the initial starting point is shown. If the player continues to struggle to follow the path, the game displays animated arrows to guide the player.

While providing visual support is a best practice, it is not always possible. Educational games in particular often have content that has

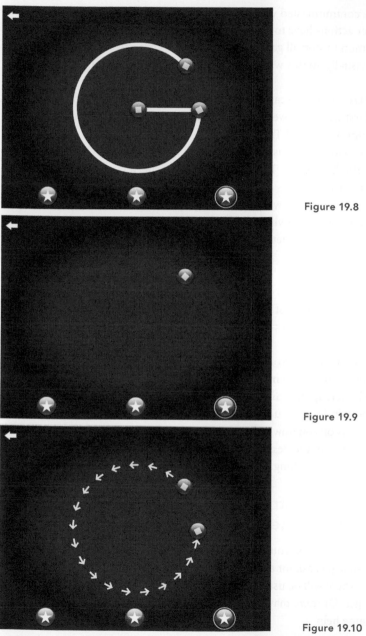

Figure 19.8

Figure 19.9

Figure 19.10

LetterSchool provides a series of visual supports to guide players to trace the letter successfully.

LetterSchool images used with permission of Sanoma Media Netherlands B.V.

to be communicated verbally, such as phonics or letter names. When player actions have to be corrected because of learning goals, it is then common to stop all gameplay and provide corrective feedback verbally and visually. In this way, the player's attention is focused on the message.

In these cases, the scaffolding structure often takes the following form.

- First wrong answer: Encourage the player to try again with verbal support: "Oops! Try again!"
- Second wrong answer: A brief verbal hint, such as "Oops! Cat begins with the letter C. Try again!" If appropriate, a visual cue can be provided as well.
- Third wrong answer: Direct the player to the correct answer with voiceover and a visual highlight of the correct answer: "Oops! Cat begins with the letter C. Pick this one!"

The risk in this design is that the voiceover can become quite lengthy, which may lead the player to disengage. Depending on the content, however, the voiceover may just need to be longer. It has to be carefully reviewed throughout the process to find the right balance of helpful and brief.

A user who gives wrong answers or appears to need help in-game can be supported in many ways. My preference is always to try to avoid interrupting gameplay whenever possible, though I certainly encounter design situations where that is not feasible or the best path. The decisions on how to support the player will always depend on the preferences of the design team. If the game is educational, the best practices for teaching the curriculum will also be a factor.

Test Your Instructions Frequently with the Target Market

As you are testing your game, you'll begin to identify the places where kids struggle, ask for additional information, or simply quit. In some cases, these will be usability problems that can be addressed with design changes. Or there may be places where you need to provide tutorials or in-game help.

Make notes of where players ask for help or where you have to explain how to play, including the actual phrasing of verbal instructions or gestures that were most helpful for the player. Then use this information to design or augment your tutorials and in-game help.

Repeat Key Instructions after Inactivity

Children have limited short-term memory. Sometimes a period of inactivity in the game can mean that the child doesn't understand what to do or has simply forgotten what to do. To be safe, repeat key instructions after a period of inactivity (generally 15–20 seconds), but keep it short. Feedback based on intervals of inactivity is called time-out feedback. If the player remains inactive for 60 seconds or more, then discontinue the time-out feedback as the player may have stepped away from the device.

Provide Visual Indications of Difficulty

In games, designers often present the difficulty of the levels explicitly, with early challenges easier than later ones. This provides a natural progression for the player to start with the easy content and move up

Figure 19.11 Visual representations of difficulty make it possible for children to select appropriate gameplay for themselves.

Little Wally Ball-y Ball image used with permission of Kids' CBC.

as she masters the gameplay. This works well with older children, who understand the concept of difficulty and are able to evaluate their own abilities and then select a level on the basis of their performance.

Designers sometimes choose to lock harder levels until the player has unlocked earlier, easier levels. When deciding whether to lock content, think about the following questions in relation to your game.

1. Does your audience understand "locked content" and will they be motivated by the challenge of unlocking it? Preschoolers, for example, are far more likely to be upset by the idea that they can't just play whatever they want to. They haven't quite grasped the construct of unlocking additional goods (remember, they're still very literal). Do you want to be the one to teach them about this?

Figure 19.12 The main menu of *Even Up Kids* displays levels that can be unlocked once the player has earned enough stars. This ensures that the player has mastered basic gameplay before moving into more difficult content.

Even Up Kids image used with permission of Simple Machine.

2. Does the game design require locked content to help the user learn particular ways of interacting with the game? Many games unlock levels as the player completes earlier puzzles. With each group of levels, new challenges are presented, such as items that hinder the player's progress. If the player could simply select any level he wanted, difficult levels would be confusing, daunting, and maddening. By controlling the player's access to levels, the game designer also scaffolds the player's experience, guiding him to the best possible outcomes.

Dynamically Adjust the Game Challenge

Game designers sometimes choose to adjust the level of difficulty dynamically behind the scenes. This adjustment may happen even in addition to allowing the parent or child to make decisions about the level of difficulty. This is not unlike a teacher-to-child interaction where a teacher evaluates the child's progress and makes decisions on how to tweak the child's experience.

For example, if you're practicing multiplication tables with a child, you might start with 2×2. If the child provides the correct answer quickly, you make a judgment that that was easy for him and "level up" to a more difficult question, such as 4×5. If you go too far, perhaps to 9×12, and the child appears to struggle by taking a long time or providing a wrong answer, you may "level down" to an easier level.

Designers can adjust the game behind the scenes using player performance metrics. This works well for younger kids, especially those who do not yet understand how to moderate difficulty for themselves. It also is a seamless way of fostering player progression, where the child continues to play without necessarily realizing that she is being evaluated.

A very simple form of scaffolding on player performance is based on whether the player answers a question correctly. The logic is basically this:

> If the answer is correct, increase question difficulty.
> If the answer is incorrect, decrease question difficulty.

Continuing with the example of helping a child learn multiplication facts, a child who answers 2×2 correctly would then be presented a more difficult question, such as 4×5. But rather than having a human making the decision, it would be predetermined by the game design.

Deciding level of difficulty question by question can be a bit jarring for the player if the level goes up and down too quickly, making the user's experience feel disjointed rather than appropriately challenging. The goal is to find the tasks that are just on the edge of the player's ability, not too easy and not too hard, just right.

One option is to change the level after a period of consistently correct or incorrect answers:

> When player has three correct answers in a row, increase question difficulty.
> When player has three incorrect answers in a row, decrease question difficulty.

Other metrics can figure into the decision as well, such as the amount of time to find the answer. The challenge is to use the metrics to identify the child's right level of difficulty. If the child has frequent incorrect answers and short response times, is he guessing and distracted? If he has frequent incorrect answers and long response times, is he mastering the task but at high risk of frustration and quitting? Do frequent correct answers and long response times mean he's at the proper level of difficulty?

Now, admittedly, this is an oversimplified breakdown of the metrics for the purpose of explaining the concept. But it shows how examining more than one metric can lead to richer information and help identify which players are likely to disengage from the content (because it's either too easy or too hard).

Using this matrix, the level logic may look more like this:

> If player has three incorrect answers in a row and average time to answer is less than five seconds, level down.
> If player has three incorrect answers in a row and average time to answer is greater than 10 seconds, do not change level.

If player has three correct answers in a row and average time to answer is less than five seconds, level up.

If player has three correct answers in a row and average time to answer is greater than 10 seconds, do not change level.

The particular decisions on when to level up and down have to be made on a case-by-case basis that's right for the particular situation. The guideline to take away here is to measure multiple dimensions to determine level scaffolding for players.

Provide Encouragement and Motivation

Developmental psychology is fraught with debates, including the debate over how much encouragement is too much and how praise should be worded. That said, everyone agrees that it's good to praise users when they're doing well and to offer encouraging words when they're struggling.

When the game has specific right and wrong answers, just as much attention should be paid to reinforcing the correct answers as to helping the user correct wrong ones. Not only does providing visual indications of success help the player understand that her actions are correct, but it also provides encouragement to continue playing.

Motivation can take many forms, including unlockable levels or content (most predictably in the form of cute clothing and accessories for the avatar), noting achievements, offering virtual currency or experience points, and providing good ol' praise with voiceover and confetti. My personal favorite success screen is *Peggle*, where cheesy visual effects are paired with Beethoven's *Ode to Joy*. It never fails to make me smile and want to play another round!

CHAPTER 20
E-books and Interactive Stories

While e-books are not necessarily games in the classic sense of the word, many include gamelike elements. They are a popular and widely requested form of digital toys for children, but, like other digital products, e-books are not without best practices for development.

E-books are not a new form of digital interactive—remember Living Books from the CD-ROM era? Over the past few decades, digital books have evolved into lushly animated and deeply interactive adventures that are wildly popular on mobile devices. Because of this rich history, you should consider a number of best practices in order to compete with the other digital books on the market.

This chapter examines types of e-books as well as best practices for developing children's e-books and interactive stories, including:
- How to model print behavior
- How to provide voiceover and visual cues for the reader
- Ways to highlight words along with narration
- Types of reading modes
- Animations and interactions that support the story
- Considerations when attempting phonics play
- Personalization in interactive stories
- Developmentally appropriate storytelling
- Fostering a love of literacy

Types of E-books

E-books offer many types of user experiences, ranging from simple to complex. A caregiver might record her own version of a story for the child to play. Or the child can play games related to the story or write a new ending to the story. The options are really limited only by technology and the development team. What follows is a brief overview of the common types of e-books.

Simple Digital E-books

The simplest form of e-book is a digital representation of the page. It is, in effect, an option to read the book on a digital device. This is akin to a Kindle-based reading experience. Simple digital e-books for kids may have color illustrations depending on the device.

Enhanced E-books

An enhanced e-book has additional tools for reading, including letting the reader hear the story read aloud. Some enhanced e-books

Figure 20.1 *Meanwhile* by Jason Shiga is a graphic novel that allows the player to follow a number of branches to different story endings. It was adapted into a mobile app as well.

Meanwhile iOS app image used with permission of Jason Shiga.

have simple animations added to some pages, which help to bring it to life.

One of my favorite e-books, which was also a print book, is *Meanwhile* by Jason Shiga. In the graphic novel, the player is given choices that lead to different paths within the story. The mobile version of the book allows the user to explore the various paths of the book as well. It's a deceptively simple design with a beautiful user experience.

Interactive E-books

Interactive e-books are full of bells and whistles. The story can be read aloud by a narrator, many objects on pages interact on touch, and the book may even include multiple story lines that the player can explore or provide additional dialogue and details that are revealed only when the reader interacts with the elements and characters on the screen. These e-books may also include games related to the story, either within the story or as additional activities.

Figure 20.2 In *Little Red Riding Hood* from Nosy Crow, the player can explore multiple paths within the story.

Image used with permission of Nosy Crow Ltd.

E-book Library (or Aggregation) Products

E-books are easily released as stand-alone products into mobile stores. Alternately, some companies are founded on a business model that creates a single product that has many books aggregated within it, such as the Reading Rainbow iPad app. In effect, these apps are digital libraries. Users then subscribe to the service to receive unlimited books, or they may pay for small collections of books.

E-book Creation Tools

While most users read and play with e-books, another important aspect of literacy learning is the ability to create text and pictures in order to tell stories. E-book creation products, such as *Scribble Press*, may include tools for writing and illustrating a story, sometimes including tools for simple animations, adding photos, or recording narration. Some apps have story prompts to help the child start the story as well. The author can usually share stories (in a safe way), either within the product or through e-mail.

Best Practices for E-books

The decision whether to use many of the following best practices depends on the degree to which your product is aiming to help support children's developing literacy skills (either in general or specific to educational standards). If the goal is to help children build literacy skills, it's very important to support as many literacy-learning behaviors as possible in the e-book, such as reading text from left to right. If your goal is entertainment and engaging storytelling, then your team may decide to give certain features lower priority.

Model Print Behaviors

E-books may be digital representations of a paper-based book, but they still offer the opportunity to model print behaviors, such as turning a page or reading from left to right. Children also need to learn the basic vocabulary of books, such as "author" and "title," and how to find that information. If the e-book has the goal of helping expose children to basic reading skills, the e-book should model relevant print behaviors.

Provide Voiceover for Text

Children generally do not become independent, confident readers until well into elementary school. Because of this, any product for children under age 10, if not older, should have audio support for any text on the page. The audio does not have to be automatically triggered, but, at a minimum, the child should have the option of pressing an icon to hear the words read aloud.

Highlight Words When They Are Read Aloud

Highlighting words as they are read, karaoke-style, is a critical feature for helping young children understand that the sounds they hear are connected with written symbols. If the goal of the product is to support this connection for emerging readers, then it is well worth the production effort to design a system that highlights the words as they are spoken aloud.

Soon the basket was packed, and Little Red Riding Hood was ready to go on her way. As she was leaving, her mother gave her a warning.

Figure 20.3 It's best practice to highlight the word as it is spoken in the narration to help reinforce children's developing literacy skills.

Little Red Riding Hood image used with permission of Nosy Crow Ltd.

Offer Varying Modes of Reading

In order to support a wide variety of reading abilities, most enhanced and interactive e-books offer multiple modes for reading the story, including "read alone" (with no narration), "read to me" (with professionally recorded narration and text highlighting), and an option that allows the reader to record the story. Some also offer a "play the story" option with additional interactive elements.

Create Animations and Interactions That Support the Story

Children are attracted to vivid production and animated elements. In e-books, the animations and interactive elements can actually affect a child's comprehension of the story. Interactive elements that highlight key story elements help reinforce a child's understanding of the story. Elements that are focused on background items that simply provide depth to the scene can detract from children's comprehension.

For example, if the sentence reads, "A bird flew to the tree," it's appropriate to animate the bird flying to the tree. But it is distracting to show clouds in the sky animating into different shapes and figures.

While elaborate and creative animations can be added to e-books, exactly what your team decides to animate should be considered against the goals of the product. If the product aims to support children's learning to read, developers should focus animations and interactions on elements that enhance and support the narration. Well-used sound and animations can also help bring a character to life.

Recognize That Phonics Are Technically Challenging

Learning letter names and letter sounds, often referred to as phonics, is an important part of learning to read. Creating tools that allow children to play with letter sounds is a great goal for a product, but it introduces a number of technical challenges.

Recording letter sounds is tedious and uses large amounts of memory size for the audio files. While there are 26 letters in English, there are many more sounds, especially when letters are combined. For educational products, the sounds have very specific pronunciations.

While we often pronounce the sound of the letter *p* as "puh," a literacy expert will deemphasize the "uh" sound and focus on just the pop sound of the letter *p*. That is a difficult sound to capture! Additionally, some sounds can be pronounced in multiple ways. Some pronounce the *wh* sound as "whuh," while other pronounce it as just "wh," which is often nearly inaudible on recording equipment.

Even once the sounds are recorded, the words that are made with the various sounds need to be recorded as well. It's not satisfying—or educationally sound—to listen to a word pronounced only as its parts. The voiceover might first pronounce "cat" as three distinct phonemes—/k/, /æ/ /t/—but to be educationally correct, the voiceover must also say the word as "cat" without separating the phonemes.

This means that the development team must also record all of the words that could be potentially created in the game. Depending on the game design, this can be quite an undertaking and use a lot of memory size. So, while phonics are an important part of literacy learning and can add a playful element to e-books, developers should be aware of the production risks and costs.

Allow Children to Personalize the Story

I earlier mentioned tools for helping children create, edit, and share stories. Additionally, allowing children to personalize stories with familiar names, images, or even sounds and recordings helps the child connect to the story. However, these personalization touches can impact other features in the e-book. For example, if you allow the child to personalize names in the story, then any prerecorded voiceover either will not work or will need to be modified. Some companies ask the player to record the name and play the recorded name as part of the voiceover. This is only as good as the actual recording made by the player. It can result in a lumpy and low-quality experience, so proceed with caution.

Tell Stories in Developmentally Appropriate Ways

Because of the animation tools available to developers, e-books frequently cross the line between video and books. It's easy to get lost in creating a beautiful experience and forget to tell the story at the child's level. So this is a reminder to tell stories in a way that is developmentally appropriate for the target audience.

For young children, that means a focus on simple stories, particularly emphasizing cause and effect. A challenging concept for young children to learn is the idea that doing one thing will cause something else to happen. Push a button to make a sound on a piano. Flip a switch to make a light turn on. Move a computer mouse to make the cursor move on a screen.

For preschoolers, storytelling is a very powerful way to communicate information, but they have limited knowledge of story sequencing, which is one reason that story sequencing shows up as an educational activity for this age. A common version of the activity presents three images to the child. In one a dog is running past a table with a vase on it. In the next, the vase is broken on the floor. In the third, the dog has run past the table and the vase is in the act of falling. The activity requires the child to put the images in the correct sequence.

As kids grow older, they become better at identifying motivations for actions, rather than simple consequences. For example, in the picture shown on page 203, a preschooler would focus on the dog jumping into the water and the fact that the dog is about to get wet. It's not until a child is older that he will be able to infer that the dog is probably jumping into the water to catch a ball, as suggested by the image of the other dog swimming with the ball in his mouth. When crafted properly, stories help children practice these skills.

Children also have to learn storytelling conventions, particularly those related to the manipulation of time. In the United States, television programs fade to black before a commercial break. This is a cue that, we have learned, means a break in the current programming. Kids must learn this convention. They also have to learn conventions of instant replays, flashbacks, and dreams. Until they have a basic mastery of time, any story convention that includes a shift in time will be difficult for the child to understand. Without this understanding, a child will think that an instant replay is the same event happening over and over again. Even once they have an understanding of time, kids have to learn the conventions, such as fade to black, that indicate a time shift.

Figure 20.4 As children grow older, they become more adept at identifying motivations for actions, rather than simply focusing on consequences. In this picture, a young child would focus on the result that the dog will get wet, whereas an older child would understand that the dog is jumping to catch a ball.

Image used under Creative Commons Attribution License by Flickr member Andrew Magill.

Foster a Love of Language and Literacy

The e-book landscape is flooded with alphabet books of all sorts of variations on "A is for . . ." But some of my favorite e-books are less about learning the specifics of letter names and more about creative uses of the technology to create digital books. For example, branching stories, such as *Meanwhile*, are a great way to encourage kids to replay the story and have an enjoyable experience with reading.

Color Uncovered is an e-book that explores the science of color through experiments and articles. It's an incredibly low-tech e-book that is well produced and that represents a great example of using technology to explain complex ideas.

Another aspect of fostering a love of literacy is supporting a child's ability to comprehend the text he is reading. When teaching comprehension to children, teachers often ask them questions around the text. The questions might ask the children to identify emotions,

Figure 20.5 *Color Uncovered* is a simple e-book that leverages technology to demonstrate concepts around the science of color.

Image used with permission of Exploratorium.

predict what will happen next, infer information from the story and illustrations, or relate the story to their personal experience.

Sample comprehension questions include:
- "The bear is crying. How is he feeling?"
- "Have you ever felt sad?"
- "What do you think is going to happen next?"
- "What words on the page begin with the letter *B*?"
- "What kinds of food is the bird eating?"

In this way, the child is prompted to think about the text as more than just sentences and illustrations.

In e-books, supporting the child in learning to do this can take multiple forms, including providing sample questions to encourage parents and caregivers to discuss the text with the child. Or the e-book may be designed so that the child has to answer questions or at least think about questions before moving on. The degree to which a product includes tools like this will always depend on the developer's educational goals as well.

CHAPTER 21
Multiplayer and Cooperative Games

Childhood is an inherently social experience. While video games are often portrayed as solo activities, games offer numerous opportunities for kids to play together with peers and caregivers, either cooperatively or competitively.

Any game that is played by two or more people, either simultaneously or asynchronously, can be considered multiplayer, whether it is cooperative or competitive in nature. For example, *Super Mario Kart* allows multiple people to simultaneously race vehicles against each other either while colocated in the same place or via an Internet connection while in

Figure 21.1 Image used under Creative Common Attribution License from Flickr member Tim Wilson.

different places. *Words with Friends*, a Scrabble-like game popular on mobile devices, is an asynchronous multiplayer game in which one player takes a turn and then waits for the other person to take a turn. *Clash of Clans* is a strategy game in which players create a village and then defend it from other players.

Kids also frequently find ways to turn games that are designed for single players into multiplayer social experiences. The simplest is by taking turns on a game that is designed for a single player. It also common for kids to turn games into parallel-play experiences. While one player is using the controller to play the game, other kids play alongside without a controller. It's especially common in dance games or other physical exertion games, such as *Dance Central*. (Search YouTube for some great videos of kids playing *Dance Central* together in this way.)

This chapter explores multiplayer games, particularly cooperative games, and includes information on fostering cooperative gameplay, particularly across generations.

Fostering Cooperative Gameplay

My favorite cooperative game is *Left 4 Dead*. It's a cooperative, first-person shooter developed for Xbox 360, as well as for Windows and Mac OS X, and released in 2008. In the game, the player controls one of four survivors of an infection that has turned the majority of humans into zombies. The player must escape various perils and move through different levels to reach safety along with the three other survivors, with whom they work throughout the game (these characters are controlled either by fellow players or AI).

Clearly this is not a game for children, but I highly suggest that any developer interested in cooperative games play the game or the sequel with three other people simultaneously. The gameplay is notable because, in order to be successful, a team must take advantage of different players' strengths in different situations and each team member must cover for others' weaknesses. When a player is hurt, the team can change formations so that someone stronger can lead. There are times when multiple players are required to win a level. In this way, communication is key to the team's success.

Despite the zombies, the game speaks to several aspects of successful cooperative strategies that are developmentally relevant for young kids. Good cooperative experiences foster communication, require more than one person to accomplish a task, create opportunities for teamwork, and allow people with different levels of skills to succeed.

Another game, one that is more age appropriate for kids, that speaks to these features is *New Super Mario Bros. Wii* (released in 2009, so you may have to hunt around for a copy). This game is the classic Super Mario side-scrolling platform game that has been around for decades, but four people can play at the same time, creating a chaotic and wonderful opportunity for cooperation.

All told, cooperative games have at least some of the following features:
- They are hard enough that more than one person is needed to complete the task.
- They encourage communication among the players, including sharing and listening to strategies.
- They allow people with different skills to shine.

In 2013, I set out to make a cooperative game for kids. It was beyond my resources to create a game like *Left 4 Dead*, but I still

Figure 21.2 The puzzles in *Williamspurrrrg* are generally too difficult for a person to solve alone. Instead, multiple players must cooperate.

Image used with the permission of No Crusts Interactive.

wanted to foster cooperation among players. The resulting game is *Williamspurrrrg HD: A Game of Cat and Mustache* for iPad. In the game, players must put mustaches and other hipster gear onto cats. In the most difficult levels, 10 items must be put onto the cats. The catch is that everything must be placed simultaneously, creating a *Twister*-like game for fingers.

Because the items in *Williamspurrrrg* have to be placed into the correct locations simultaneously, it is nearly impossible for some levels to be solved by one person, so players turn to others for help. To solve the levels, they have to coordinate their movements, which fosters communication among the players. The game design fosters cooperation by creating opportunities for interaction between players.

Designing for Intergenerational Interaction

Games have a reputation for being solo experiences; a common belief is that caregivers use games (or video) as digital babysitters, implying that caregivers are not present during the child's interactions with technology. I strongly encourage parents and caregivers to play with kids whenever possible. It allows them an opportunity to connect with the child over something the child enjoys, and it also gives the caregiver an opportunity to draw connections to other activities and interests.

The challenge, however, is that children's media can be intensely boring (or annoying) for adults, especially when the child is young. The following are considerations for developers who aim to design for intergenerational audiences.

Create Tools and Games for Everyday Interactions

Games can provide powerful motivation for everyday interactions and activities as well as opportunities for groups of people to use technology together. One way to accomplish this is to take common actions and structure a game around them. Chores are perhaps the most salient opportunity for games in children's lives, and several companies have made games in this space. For example, *Chore Wars* is structured as a role-playing game in which each member of the

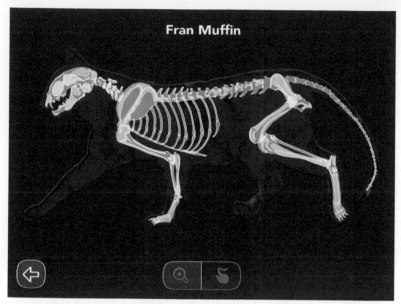

Fran Muffin

Figure 21.3 *Dr. PetPlay* transforms a tablet into a tool for giving animals (stuffed and real) a check-up, including logging the animal's symptoms, weight, and temperature and viewing x-rays.

Image used with permission of Pretendasaurus.

household is a character who receives experience points for every chore completed.

While not a game, another option that fosters interaction is tools that parents can use with the child, such as toothbrush timers or bedtime tools. In *Sleepasaurus,* the child helps put a dinosaur to sleep. The parent can set the time when the dinosaur wakes up, providing a visual indication of when the child can get out of bed. (This is incredibly helpful before kids know how to tell time!)

Or interactive activities can become part of the toolset kids use to play, such as *Toca Tea Party*, which provides a virtual tea set, or *Dr. PetPlay*, which turns the iPad into a tool for giving stuffed animals a check-up. A child can play with a parent, a friend, or even her stuffed animal collection. These kinds of experiences, regardless of whether they are games in the classic sense, allow families (or kids in a classroom) to collaborate and cooperate.

Aim for Dual-Premise Writing and Design

When an adult watches *Sesame Street* skits and finds himself laughing along with "Upside Downton Abbey," "Rhyme Scene Investigator," or "Cookie Monster in the Hungry Games," that's because the writers are doing what's known as dual-premise writing. The jokes are funny on two levels—for the child as well as for the adult. The adult humor flies right over the head of the child, while the child simultaneously sees her favorite characters doing things that are funny to her. Everyone is happy. Many family-friendly programs strive to be funny on multiple levels.

Game designers can use this idea of dual-premise writing for the content, but they can also work toward that goal in the game design.

One of the best examples is *Super Mario Galaxy*, which is a 3D version of the classic platform game for Nintendo Wii. Player 1 has the task of navigating the world. If desired, a second player can play along simultaneously but has a far simpler task. Player 2 points the Wii remote at the screen to control a cursor that collects star bits on the screen.

If two adults play *Super Mario Galaxy* together in this way, it may not be a very compelling cooperative experience. But if an adult and a child play together, it creates a really nice opportunity for the parent to play the game at his skill level while the child plays at a skill level appropriate to her.

Games such as *Dance Dance Revolution* and *Rock Band* also allow players to pick the skill level appropriate for each person. So one person can be playing on a harder level while another person plays at an easier one. These are games based around ageless, universal, enjoyable activities—playing music and dancing—that families do together all the time, and they allow each person to play at his own level.

Offer Tools for Creating Games Together

A number of tools are available for creating games or game worlds. Perhaps the most popular is *Minecraft*, which is a sandbox game, one in which players can roam freely through a virtual world. At the simplest level, *Minecraft* is about using blocks to build. But it has been used to create incredibly elaborate worlds and structures. Because they create a virtual world, players have the option to socialize in the world. Many

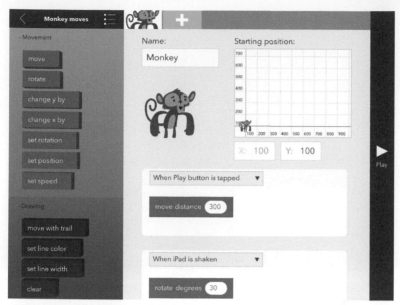

Figure 21.4 *Hopscotch: Coding for Kids* is an age-appropriate toolset to help younger children learn the basics of programming.

Image used with permission of Hopscotch Technologies.

kids spend time socializing in *Minecraft*, even while sitting next to each other in the same room.

Minecraft is one of the numerous tools that allow people to connect via a game. Software development tools to use in creating games are also common. The programs vary wildly in difficulty. *GameMaker* and *GameSalad* are popular ones that can be used casually but that also allow developers to release professionally produced games.

Other tools are produced specifically to teach kids the basics of programming; these include *Scratch* and *Hopscotch: Coding for Kids*. These programs have a rich history of classroom use and have supporting documentation for those who wish to introduce the product to kids.

It's also common for games to release toolsets that allow players to create their own levels. *Scribblenauts, Portal 2,* and *Little Big Planet* all include these tools, and all are opportunities for social interactions and collaboration, which are dynamics enjoyed by both kids and adults.

CHAPTER 22
Player Data in Games and Progress Tracking

The interconnected nature of today's devices makes tracking children's progress through games and reporting their progress an attractive feature. It also means that data can be incorporated into the gameplay itself. But these features are not without challenges, including how to legally handle the data collected from children.

This chapter discusses gathering and utilizing user data for children, including:
- Privacy considerations for children
- Integrating data into gameplay
- Badges and achievements
- Reporting progress for parents and caregivers

Managing Children's Personal Data

Before delving into the opportunities for tracking children's progress over time, we need to note one important caveat—the territory or country for which you are developing your game may have rules for how to handle personal data for children.

For example, in the United States, developers have to comply with the Children's Online Privacy Protection Act, or COPPA. This law provides guidelines for companies that are collecting personal information from children under age 13, such as name, birthday, or address. It provides guidelines for how the company must secure permission from a caregiver in order to collect and store the data and requires that the data be deleted on request or when the child leaves the service.

The laws and their interpretation shift as technology evolves. Before releasing a product, consult a qualified professional opinion (e.g., a lawyer familiar with the laws of the particular country) on whether there are additional steps you must take.

Data as a Part of the Gameplay

Our society is increasingly data driven, which in turn drives the need for kids to learn to interpret and use data in their everyday lives. The

Figure 22.1 *Perfect Slice* challenges the player to draw a line that divides an object perfectly in half. Once the player draws the line, the game provides feedback on how well he did, including showing the actual percentage on each side of the line, such as 43.2% on one side and 56.8% on the other.

Image used with permission of Curious Bit.

ability to collect, organize, and understand data visualizations is an educational goal within STEM curricula. Games provide a natural opportunity for players to practice with data of all sorts. Some of my favorites include *Perfect Slice*, *Eyeballing Game*, and *QatQi*, all of which are shown in this chapter. These games represent a few of the many ways that data and data visualizations can become part of the activity.

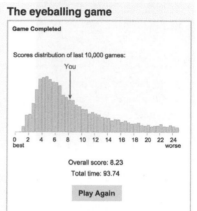

Figures 22.2–22.3 The online game called the *Eyeballing Game* challenges players on a series of geometric tasks, including finding the midpoint of a line and finding the center of a circle. The player is given three attempts at each task and is scored on accuracy and time. Once the game ends, a histogram provides visual feedback of how the player scores relative to everyone else.

Images used with permission of Mattias Wandel.

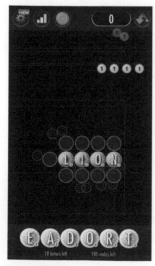

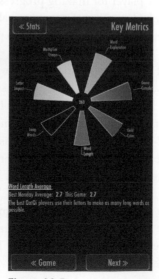

Figure 22.4   **Figure 22.5**

Figure 22.6

Figures 22.4–22.6 *QatQi* is a word game that provides a number of statistics to compare the player's performance to that of players in the same region as well as around the world. (Figures 22.4 to 22.6.)

QatQi images used with permission of Zworkbench.

Badges and Achievements in Gameplay

One of the most compelling ways to use player progress data is to simply reward the player for making progress through the game with achievements or badges. These features can also provide powerful motivation to encourage kids to continue to play the game.

An easy form of this that is popular in games is to award stars for how well the player solved the level. If the player solves the level perfectly, she receives the full number of stars. Games like *Cut the Rope* and *Angry Birds* use this structure, as do many kids games, such as Kids' CBC *Little Wally Ball-y Ball*. It provides an easy visual way for the child to understand that she has mastered the level or that she can continue to practice that level and achieve the full score.

Assigning value to the stars in order to assign a degree of perfection, however, can be a difficult task. Is it based on accuracy? How long it took to solve the puzzle? Number of moves? In the case of the *Little*

Figure 22.7 A common technique in games is to provide a number of stars (or similar icon) as a reflection of how well the player performed in the level.

Little Wally Ball-y Ball image used with permission of Kids' CBC.

Wally Ball-y Ball game, the criterion is a measure of how many stars the player picked up while solving the puzzles. All of this is to say that stars, or any similar award, can feel arbitrary if the award is not carefully designed to be aligned with the goals of the game.

At one point not so long ago, it seemed every action I took digitally might earn me a badge. Deposit a check? Achievement! Order lunch twice from the same restaurant? Badge! Reach level 10? Achievement!

Thank goodness, the achievement and badge fever, often referred to as gamification, is calming, which let us talk about the right places to use badges and achievements to foster motivation or to provide nuanced information and feedback.

Badges are traditionally a sign of mastery or progress. Think about the Girl or Boy Scouts and badges. You earn badges for mastering skills. Some are easier to earn than others, but they're not awarded without effort on the Scout's part. They're also not awarded for behaviors that the Scout would generally be doing anyway.

In other words, I don't need a badge for depositing 10 checks. I have sufficient motivation to deposit them! You can be sure that I'm going to deposit those checks regardless of whether I receive an award. The motivation is already built in—I'd like to put the money in my bank account! But if my bank wants to encourage me to use its app to deposit the money, a well-designed achievement or rewards system might encourage me to try its new system.

This is in contrast to an experience like Foursquare, in which players check in at the places they go. If a person checks in at a place most often, he becomes the mayor of that location, which is a reward for some. You don't need a badge for going to your favorite restaurant repeatedly, but there are bragging rights that come with becoming the mayor. In that sense, Foursquare provides motivation for those who find value in that activity.

The challenge in designing badges and achievements is to define the behaviors that are most aligned with the goals of the game as well as those that are most interesting to the players. Otherwise, the risk is that the achievements will simply reward behaviors that the player would do anyway, rather than challenging them.

One of my absolute favorite examples of in-game achievements is *Plants vs Zombies*. In this game, the player is defending a house from attacking zombies. The player must spend resources to "buy" plants for the front lawn. These plants, in turn, kill the zombies. The currency used to buy plants is suns, which fall at regular intervals. During normal gameplay, the player will spend suns almost as quickly as he earns them in order to keep a solid defense against the zombies.

Plants vs Zombies has a large list of achievements. (It should be noted that I'm talking specifically about the original *Plants vs Zombies* game, not the sequel.) Many challenge the player to do something that's hard to do, such as using only one kind of plant to win a level, rather than mixing and matching to get the best defense.

My favorite is the Sunny Days Achievement. As I mentioned, in normal play you spend the in-game currency of suns almost as quickly as you earn it in order to kill the zombies as quickly as possible. I rarely have more than 200 suns when I'm playing. But the Sunny Days Achievement requires that the player earn 3,000 suns; this causes a complete reversal of strategy. Rather than killing zombies as quickly as possible, the player switches to killing them slowly (but not so slowly as to lose!) in order to earn that many suns.

This is a great example of an achievement that encourages the player to change his behavior and to think about strategy. It's not just about rewarding the regular behavior or rewarding those who play a lot. Achievements can be a powerful way of encouraging players to try new strategies and behaviors.

Reporting Progress to Parents and Caregivers

When the game or activities are educationally focused, some developers create tools for reporting the child's progress, such as what topics he covered or how well he performed on the tasks. How much information

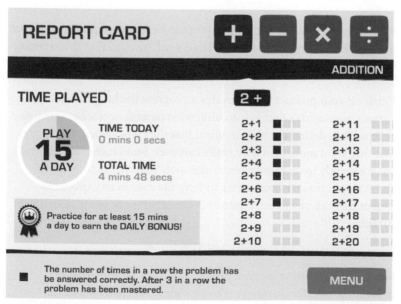

Figure 22.8 *Medieval Math Battle* provides a detailed dashboard that records the number of times the player has answered individual math equations.

Image used with permission of Spinfall.

the progress report provides depends greatly on the depth of the actual experience. For example, *TeachMe Toddler* provides a fairly brief overview, whereas *Medieval Math Battle* provides a log of every math equation the child has answered.

Progress reports seem like a really logical and good idea. Even parents and teachers will tell you that they want to know what their child is doing. However, the reality is that these tools are rarely used. Some are too complicated; parents want an at-a-glance view. Many require the parent to log into a system, which is asking a lot of busy parents.

Another challenge is that progress dashboards generally report what the child is doing (equations answered) rather than what the child is learning (e.g., basic addition). Parents and teachers often want the latter, but it's far more complicated to determine if the child is actually learning. The test learning scientists often use is whether a learned concept can be applied in another environment. So while the child may be able to answer basic addition questions in a game, can she transfer her knowledge to paper in class or use it in a conversation?

If your product requires helping parents and caregivers understand what the child is learning, educational advisers will be critical in determining that the learning methods implemented in the game are sound.

Finally, if your product plan includes a progress tracking dashboard for parents, spend extra time researching what parents or teachers are using or what they desire (but keep in mind that they'll be biased, telling you that they want more than they really can use). Build incrementally and test frequently to make sure you create tools that will be truly useful. For example, teachers may prefer to have the data in an exportable format that can be imported into another program or easily shared with parents.

Extension Activities for Parents and Caregivers

Rather than reporting detailed progress metrics, another option in creating tools for caregivers is to provide contextual and useful information to extend the activities beyond the game.

The activity might still track and report what the child does, such as what letters she played with, but then the software might additionally recommend activities the parent can do with the child. In the case of letters, this provides an opportunity for the parent to draw connections along the lines of "You played with the letter p today in the game! Let's look for the letter p at the grocery store."

Even if the activity does not specifically tie the child's activity to extension activities, it's good practice to provide additional information for the parent to reinforce the curriculum of the product.

CHAPTER 23
Marketing for Kids and Families

Prepare yourself. Marketing is a lot of work and is critical to the success of your game. You cannot just release the game into the wild and expect it to magically rocket to success.

Making a product for children and families is an amazing feeling. It's for the children! It's funny! It's got cute characters! Kids can learn! You feel like a superhero because you've made this amazing game.

And then it's released into the world. And I know that every single one of us secretly dreams of the amazing traffic, the reviews, the reception, and the accolades that the game will bring.

Almost everyone—I'd argue 99 percent of developers—feel a crushing moment when they realize that the digital product marketplaces are brutal, particularly in the kids' space. Advertising options are limited. Some of the most successful monetization strategies, such as free-to-play, are really difficult to implement ethically and safely. With parents expecting free or incredibly inexpensive prices and hundreds of thousands of products available, it's hard to make a mark, never mind turn a profit.

So that puts a lot of pressure on marketing and outreach campaigns. This chapter explores considerations for marketing children's games, including:
- Defining success metrics
- Building a brand
- Engaging the customer
- Starting marketing during development
- Guidelines for marketing materials
- Public relations

Defining Success Metrics

I'm a data nerd. I love measuring anything and everything I can. Marketing is no different. To help you be successful in your campaigns, I recommend clearly defining measurable success metrics that are relevant to your business and then focusing like a laser on those metrics.

Any number of things can serve as a success metric. These are common options:

- Purchases (or downloads if your product is free): The number of times your product has been purchased gives you a measure of how word is spreading.
- Engagement: If you have user behavior tracking ability, time spent with your content provides information on what's connecting with your user and what needs additional work.
- Ratings: Ratings and reviews can mean better performance in many of the marketplaces. They also provide a glimpse into what your users like and dislike about the product.
- Repeat users: As with engagement, knowing whether your users come back to your content provides information on what's sticky and worth further investigation.
- Social signals: Are your users spreading the word via social media channels? This metric should likely be further divided into specific signals, such as Facebook likes, Twitter mentions, Pinterest pins, and so on. You could also look at the quality of the type of mentions you're receiving. Are they positive or negative?
- Press mentions: The number of press mentions as well as the quality of the periodical that gives you a mention is another way to track your product's traction.
- E-mail list sign-ups: If you plan to sell more product, converting your users into a list is an easy way to spread the word down the road.

It's tempting to pick all of these as critical metrics. In reality, you should keep an eye on all of them, but making each one a priority will split your attention too far. Instead, pick two that make the most sense for your business. If you have the luxury of partners or employees who can monitor other metrics, do so. Having more information can lead to smarter decisions.

Personally, I used to focus on purchases and social signals. Purchases are important because you're running a business. Purchases mean $$, which funds new products, which must make $$ in order to fund new products. . . .

But recently, I've replaced purchased with a focus on e-mail list sign-ups. When I'm releasing new products, it's important to me to have a significant list to whom to market my product, which will convert into sales. In flooded marketplaces such as those we have now, the ability to speak directly to the customer is priceless. Additionally, word of mouth (or social sharing) is the other metric that I watch carefully.

Once you choose success metrics, you also have to set goals and timeframes for achieving them, and you have to hold yourself to them.

If you don't set goals, you'll rationalize whatever sales you do have.

"We sold three apps yesterday! Hooray!"

Is that actually something to celebrate? Only if your goal was to sell three a day. But if your goal was 10 apps per day, then it's not a success.

A simple goal to try is to increase downloads by 10 percent within a defined timeframe: Sell 10 percent more apps each month. Sign up 10 percent more people each week. Or set a goal to reach out to five reporters each week. Or post to Twitter twice a day.

Then hold yourself to the goals. Write them down, tell a trusted friend or colleague, and update on the progress. Research shows that people accomplish goals 33 percent more if they write them down and share the information.

By following the metrics and understanding the data you collect, you quantify your experiments and can tweak your overall strategy. It helps you stay resilient for the long haul. That data trail also helps you demonstrate how thoughtful and disciplined you are when you pursue funding, grants, or partnerships down the road.

Approach Your Brand as If It Were a Record Label

The reality of the children's media business is that many of us are supporting multiple brands or at least multiple products at once. Rarely do we have the opportunity to focus wholly on a single product and then move to the next one.

Often, each product or property requires an additional Facebook page, Twitter account, website, and all the fixings. Managing all those sites is hard enough for a single property, but managing all of those things for multiple products becomes a daunting, nearly impossible task.

Because of this, I recommend that, whenever possible, companies approach their products as if they were part of a record label, where everything clearly fits within an umbrella brand, rather than as a series of individual products.

Record labels are amazing at consistency. Once you're a fan of Def Jam Recordings, you know that you can purchase any of its products and get a particular kind of music experience and quality. Authors and book imprints have the same kind of following. Once you're a fan of an author, you'll buy his books faithfully. Similarly, there's a reason book trilogies and series have become so popular—it's far easier for a publisher to market a series than to launch a new author. Once you're a fan of the first book, brand recognition will carry through for additional books.

If you start over from scratch for each new book, it's much harder to build an audience. By thinking of your products as a suite of games within a larger brand, you can carry your loyal audience from product to product.

Many indie game studios (outside the children's space), such as Owlchemy Labs and Dejobaan Games, successfully do this. Even though their individual games may not be of the same genre, they're all part of the company brand. Fans of one game will engage in another game from the developer because they've become fans of the developer.

Look at Nick Jr. or PBS KIDS. They're also made up of lots of little brands, but they have built trust for the umbrella brand, so when they launch a new product within their brand it has a built-in following. That product will grow its own following, too, over time, but it has the benefit of being associated with the larger brand to start.

So, as you build your own games and products, keep an eye on developing the umbrella brand and treat it as if it were the record industry. Think about your products as a suite within a larger brand, and use that brand to engage a loyal following.

Engage the Customer Personally

We generally set out to be as efficient as possible in our marketing efforts. Why reach out to an individual when I can e-mail 100 at once?

When building a brand or launching a marketing campaign, the best thing you can do is forget the idea of reaching as many people a day as you possibly can. Replace it with a goal of engaging individual customers. Perhaps your goal is to engage the first 100 customers personally. Or to reach out to five people a day to explain about the product and ask for feedback.

Reaching as many people as possible leads to a spamming mindset. It's also easy for the recipient to ignore a mass message. Reaching out to people personally (and not just with a template message) puts recipients on their best behavior. They are far more likely to respond to a personal request than to a generalized call for help. It's the polite thing to do!

I completely acknowledge that this is not a scalable tactic. At some point you will not be able to keep up and will have to prioritize or delegate. But you will not be sorry for spending time and energy on engaging customers personally. You might get a sale from the person, a new e-mail subscriber, or some feedback, or the recipients might spread the word to their networks. At a larger level, you'll begin to foster a culture of personal service that goes a long way toward building a trusted brand.

Remember, building these kinds of businesses is a marathon, not a sprint (or whatever metaphor you want to use). Keep your metrics in mind and chip away at the goals.

Start Marketing during Product Development

A lot of developers work steadfastly at making their product, then, about a week or so before launch, ask, "How are we going to market this?" It's probably too late if you put yourself in that position.

Marketing really should begin as early as possible, ideally as soon as you decide your game is viable. I might even argue that your confidence in your ability to market the game should be part of the decision whether your game is viable.

Once you are fairly confident you will be shipping a game, start preparing the marketing campaign, including these tasks:

- Become a master of search engine optimization (SEO) and keywords. (The Internet has lots of resources for SEO. See the appendix for suggestions.)
- If it is appropriate for the age of your audience, plan to embed the code for social media sharing (e.g., the ability to post to Facebook or Twitter from within the game), analytics, and, if relevant, tools for prompting the user to rate your product into the game.
- Track competitor mentions for intel on their performance, press leads, and other possible competitors. Google Alerts is a simple tool for this.
- Start building (or continue to nurture) your editorial connects at the relevant marketplaces (e.g., Apple App Store) and press outlets. But don't be annoying.
- If development has reached a point where you're comfortable demonstrating the product, give small demos to help build interest.
- Engage your social media by providing useful links and information. Some developers very freely share information about products in development to help build interest and engage the audience.

Marketing Materials and Guidelines

In a market so crowded with great products, your marketing materials should be carefully crafted.

Be Ridiculously Clear in Your Message

It's the old elevator pitch argument. (The elevator pitch is the amount of information you can convey in an average elevator ride, around 30 seconds or so.) If you can't say the goal of your product succinctly, how can your marketing materials do so?

If you clearly defined your goals (e.g., purchases), this will help guide what language and imagery you use on the marketing materials. Explain exactly what your product does, what problems it solves (or what skills it augments, as may be the case in education), and how it fits into the audience's life.

Focus your website on getting people to download your content. Remove anything else that's not in immediate service of your goals. Don't clog the homepage with messages about t-shirts and other stuff (unless that's actually your goal).

Crafting Descriptions for Online Marketplaces

If you review descriptions of games on the various marketplaces, you'll notice that most fall into a formula. The majority of descriptions boil down to the following categories of information, generally in this order:

- Brag (e.g., quotes, reviews, awards). If your app is on sale for a reduced price, include that here.
- Pithy summary (think tweet-length).
- Tips for successful play (if needed). You should already know if you need this based on user testing or previous reviews.
- Additional longer descriptive points (optional).
- Features in bulleted-list form. Anything goes, including types of puzzles, who made the music, audience information, and so on. Some promotions separate game features from educational features.
- Additional information about the developer and/or cross-promotion.
- Privacy policy information and other legalese (if needed).

Here is an example of a game description that uses this formula. Like most marketing materials, the description is a living document. So plan to update and tweak descriptions regularly.

It is a truth universally acknowledged that Stride & Prejudice is an unusual endless runner where the platforms are made from the text of Pride and Prejudice.

> "A clever literary twist." Pocket Gamer
> "It's a really clever concept." TouchArcade
> "I love the fact that this exists." Stuart Dredge, *The Guardian*
> "5 Stars." GameInformer
> "A fun little mobile game." Macworld
> "Society is finally getting the endless-running adaptation of a literary classic that it deserves." VentureBeat

Features
* Run as a pixel-art rendition of Lizzy Bennet, fashionably dressed in high heels and an empire-waisted dress!

* Marathon mode challenges you to see how far you can go when always starting from the beginning.

* Reader mode is for picking up where you fell off so you can read the entire book.

* Customize the speed of scrolling and the color scheme for maximum eye comfort, including white text on black, black text on white, or sepia. Just like your Kindle app!

* It's universal for all your devices, including iPhone, iPad, and iPod touch.

Stride & Prejudice is brought to you by No Crusts Interactive, where we create family-friendly games that blend progressive educational philosophies with innovative game mechanics. You can reach us at info@NoCrusts.com or @NoCrusts on Twitter.

This game does not use in-app purchases or third-party advertising.

An Image Is Worth 1,000 Words

No matter how long you labor over the description of your product, most customers will make snap judgments based on the marketing images, particularly in the app stores, where images are given a dominant placement. These images have to clearly communicate what the game is about in an eye-catching way.

I personally have made the mistake of being cute and cheeky in marketing instead of focusing on the message. When I first released Williamspurrrrg for iPad, I made marketing images that were funny and not at all informative. I received messages from strangers who suggested I edit the images because, even after reading the description, "they didn't know what the game was about."

I kept the funny images but replaced the text with specific information that described the game.

It's also a good idea to have at least one image that shows children (and adults if relevant) playing the game. It's a subtle message that will reinforce the idea that kids enjoy playing your game. But do this only if you have a high-quality image (and make sure you have permission to use the kids in the photo).

Figures 23.1–23.2 Marketing images from *Williamspurrrrg HD: A Game of Cat and Mustache*. The first image (Figure 23.1) left people wondering what the game was about, while the second (Figure 23.2) kept the humor of the game while providing information.

Images used with permission of No Crusts Interactive.

If you're doing the marketing material yourself, refer to resources on designing marketing materials. Also look to the successful companies to see how they're handling design. Don't limit yourself to only the children's space, but rather study major companies that likely have money to spend on professional marketing and see what you can take away from their examples.

One of my favorite bits of marketing wisdom is the eye gaze effect, which is a psychological phenomenon in which humans follow the gaze of humans, even when the people are in pictures. It's why you automatically look up when you see someone else look up. Study marketing images and you'll notice that if the people in the ads are not looking at the camera, they're looking at an important part of the ad, such as the logo.

Figure 23.3 Humans naturally follow the gaze of other humans, even in photos, which can be a powerful tool in marketing.

Image used under Creative Commons Attribution License from Flickr member David Amsler.

Have a Video Trailer

Video trailers help consumers "try out" content. Professional reviewers also frequently embed game trailers in their published reviews alongside their own review. When this happens, you're helping to shape what message is sent to the readers. Additionally, when combined with proper search engine optimization techniques, video trailers tend to have high search engine placement.

Post your video to a site that enables embedded views, such as YouTube or Vimeo. This way you can easily embed the video in your own materials. Press sites and reviewers can also easily embed the video in their own materials.

Create a Digital Press Kit

No doubt you've heard of press kits before. A press kit for a game generally includes a press release and high-res screenshots of the game. If you have a video trailer, you should include a link to it in your press kit.

Make sure your press release follows basic best practices. The Web is full of resources on how to write a good press release, even those specific to games. If you're unsure how to write the release, have friends and colleagues review it in advance or hire a professional to write it for you. A number of freelance public relations consultants offer this service.

One of my favorite examples of a simple and straightforward online press kit is the one created for the game *Hundreds*. It features a description of the game, a video, screenshots, a list of awards and press received, and information on the team.

Brand Screenshots with Your Logo

Some games offer a feature that allows players to save a photo of their work. This is especially common in activities where the child is creating content, such as *Elmo's Monster Maker*. When the player saves the image, make sure your logo is added to the image so that when the player shares the content, you benefit from the exposure.

Humans Share Materials That Foster Emotion, Particularly Interest, Surprise, and Amusement

It's a basic human condition. We share stuff that makes us feel emotion, particularly the emotions of interest ("Oh, I didn't know that"), surprise ("What? No way!"), and amusement (anything that makes you LOL). Anger is another emotion that gets shared a lot, but it is less useful for marketing.

Look through your Facebook or Twitter feeds and see how many of the posts fall into these categories. BuzzFeed and SlideShare are excellent resources for exploring how well-crafted headlines and descriptions foster emotions as well as social sharing.

Build Trust and Awareness for Your Brand by Participating in Conversations around the Internet

Well before you launch a product, you can start building trust in your brand by becoming an information resource. Perhaps you've heard reports that Twitter posts that share information are retweeted more often than self-promotional posts. You can use this to your advantage— use your brand's Twitter account to share materials (and keep it surprising, interesting, and amusing!). You'll gain trust as a resource and have a following once time comes to promote your materials.

Another option is to actively participate in blog discussions and resource sites such as Quora and Hacker News. Or you might write a guest blog for a gaming or media site, where you can share more about the development of the game and your experience. Any of these activities will also help boost your search engine optimization.

It's best to start participating in these communities long before your product launches so that you can build a reputation with relevant communities. Aim to become useful and provide helpful information without ever being asked. Then, when time comes to call in your favors, you'll already have some karma points built up.

Carefully Select Your Social Media Presence and Update It Regularly

We have a lot of social media options available these days—Facebook, Twitter, Pinterest, Google+, and so on. The temptation is to give your brand a presence on every option possible—not to mention that many people will argue that your website should have a blog as well.

Just as I argued that you should not launch a new set of social media sites for each new product, I also urge you to limit how many social media channels you use for your brand in general and to set a strict schedule for when you update the sites. It does not reflect well on your brand when the site hasn't been updated recently, whether it's a blog, Facebook page, or otherwise. It also doesn't reflect well if the site has only a few followers.

To decide what's relevant for you, first ask how much time you can reasonably spend updating the materials. Then examine where your target audience is most likely to spend time – Facebook? Twitter? E-mail newsletter? Use your competitors to help inform this decision. Then invest the time and energy to grow the users and post regularly. If you find yourself not using a social media outlet, decide whether it's time to push the delete button.

Submit Your Game for Reviews

As previously mentioned, people greatly trust the word of other people. So an important part of the marketing strategy is to collect reviews and ratings, from both professionals and your audience. Tracking your competitors' press mentions will help you identify review sites.

Professional Reviews

Reaching professional reviewers in a crowded marketplace can be very difficult. But children's games are reviewed and featured in a wide variety of places with reviews by various commenters, from professional news sources to independent bloggers.

If you're in the position to work with a public relations team, a large focus of their efforts will be to generate positive reviews. To reach reviewers, try the following methods:

- Follow the review site's instructions for how to submit a game. Many will have a "tips@ . . . " e-mail address or a submission form.
- E-mail reviewers directly. A little bit of searching will often yield e-mail addresses for the people you're interested in contacting.

- Ask friends and colleagues for introductions to reviewers. Demo the game for your friends first so that they can pass along their own endorsement to the reviewer.
- Many reviewers attend conferences. If you recognize a reviewer, approach him. Have your best elevator pitch ready and offer to demo the game. (Many reviewers will ask you to send the game, and you should respect that.) Ask for a business card and make sure you follow up. Make sure you approach reviewers in appropriate situations. Do not pitch in the bathroom. (You'd be shocked how often this happens.)
- Use LinkedIn to connect with reviewers.

If you have a press kit, send the link to the reviewers. If you're e-mailing or connecting with them online, write a targeted e-mail. Reviewers can sniff out a template submission, so try at least to tailor the beginning of the message. (Think of it as a variation on reaching out to your users individually.)

Professional review submissions frequently cost money. Some reviewers ask for an administration fee to cover the costs of reviewing products. Some charge for expedited reviews. Others will post a review for free but charge to promote their review on Facebook or other social media services. To determine whether it is worth the fees, examine the potential exposure of the review:

- Is the review site a long-standing, trusted brand?
- Does the site share statistics on how many impressions or page views the average review receives?
- Have respected colleagues used the site before?
- Does your product fit the profile of games the site usually reviews? (In other words, don't submit an iPhone game to a PC gaming site.)

This is all information to help you gauge whether the traffic is high enough quality to be worth the cost.

User (Amateur) Reviews and Ratings

Amateur or user reviews, such as those that appear in app stores, are important both for word of mouth and for rankings within the game marketplaces. While the exact algorithms marketplaces use to rank the products are secret, it's long been understood that the number of

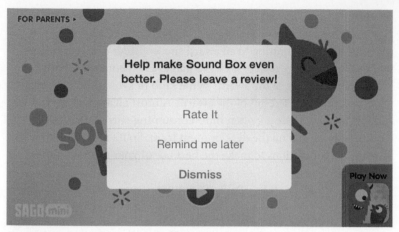

Figure 23.4 Reviews are important to the marketing success of a game, so many developers embed a review request in their products.

Sago Mini Sound Box image used with permission from Sago Sago.

reviews as well as average ratings (e.g., 4 out of 5 stars) are part of the equation.

Many games embed a request to the user to review the game. Whether you can do this depends on the age of your audience and the level of trust you have with the audience. Some parents will be bothered that you displayed a link that will take the child out of the game experience, but most will tolerate a one-time request.

Some developers also embed a link that lets you rate the game in the information or credits part of the game. It's a subtle request but may be more appropriate if you're making a game for very young players.

If you distribute your game digitally (e.g., via an app store), be mindful that when you update, the new version number you choose could "reset" your reviews. For example, major version updates (such as from Version 1.1 to Version 2.0) will triggers the Apple App Store to hide your ratings until you receive enough new ratings for the new version. Smaller updates (from Version 1.0.0 to 1.0.1) generally do not cause you to have to start over. Consult with your programmer when you're deciding what to name the version update.

Awards

Like professional review sites, awards can be good or bad. When you are considering submitting to an award site, consider criteria similar to those for choosing review sites. Do games like yours tend to win? What's the following of the award? What kind of promotion have past winners received as a result of the award? Almost all awards carry application fees. There are often time-consuming entry forms that require information on the development team. So it's important to work through these questions to make the best use of your time and funds.

Games and Public Relations Agencies

A question that you will inevitably face is whether to use a public relations agency or consultant in your publicity efforts. PR agencies are expensive, in part because they generally require a three-month contract. It takes time for the agency to reach out to contacts and cultivate the best stories for your brand, so it's understandable that it needs to have some runway to work with.

PR agencies also have significant contacts already in place, so if you're new to the field or have not been able to spend much time working your network prior to the release of the game, PR professionals can be a huge help.

It often comes down to a question of what you can afford and your goals. If you're unsure, talk with a few PR companies and see if you find one that offers a reasonable price and approach for your product. A number of companies know that developers are cash sensitive, and some offer discount services in which they will simply write the press releases or send a press release to a distribution list.

Summary

All told, marketing, regardless of what audience you're serving, is about relationships with the customers. If you read any of the leading books on marketing, you'll realize that marketing is psychology, the art of fostering emotions that cause the customer to purchase your product and spread the word. You'll do all of these things in the places where your audience spends time—if they're parents, you'll be on Facebook, Pinterest, or Twitter; if they're teens, you'll be on Vine and Instagram. And so on.

Making a Game

Image used with the permission of the author.

It's one of the most common questions I hear: "How do I make a game?" Such a small question with such a big answer! This book wouldn't be so dense (nor would it exist!) if it were an easy-to-answer question. All of the preceding chapters provide a road map for development.

But to make it a little easier, in conclusion, here are some parting thoughts on how to use all of the material in this book in one cohesive plan. Note that while this information is in linear order, a good development process is generally active in more than one area, if not in all areas at the same time, or you will find yourself returning to various parts regularly. For example, competitive analysis is never really done; you should always keep an eye on your competition. It's a cycle, not a step-by-step process.

Familiarize Yourself with the Market and Your Audience

The children's market has hundreds of thousands of digital products available across all the various platforms, be it Web, mobile app, console game, or otherwise. It's a crowded, competitive space. That means there's a very high probability that someone has already made the product you're thinking about or something very, very, very similar to it. And it would be very sad to waste any of your hard-earned dollars on something someone else has already made.

Section One of this book is about familiarizing yourself with the business of designing games. Use the guidelines in chapter 7 to help you perform a competitive analysis and identify opportunities in the market. Then use the chapters in Section Two to familiarize yourself with the basic needs of your target audience.

Design, Develop, Test, Iterate

Once you establish that your idea has a competitive chance, it's time to begin the design process. As part of this, you should select your business model and make any other business decisions, such as creating a budget or choosing a platform.

The design process should ideally be a mix of building and testing repeatedly. It's a very iterative process that starts with the smallest reasonable bit and then grows with each stage. This is a period when designers may be tempted to hire someone to storyboard the entire experience. I caution against that, especially if you're fairly new to game design and production. If you design everything on paper and then just build that, you'll likely find yourself making expensive changes late in the design cycle, if you can make the changes at all.

Related to this idea, here are four points that can be difficult to keep in mind during development but that are quite important factors in the success of a design process. These points closely parallel best practices in entrepreneurship.

1. *Business plans and game design documents are living, breathing documents.*

These documents throw a stake in the ground, but they are not the absolute truth of the project. It used to be that the business plan was the ultimate five-year plan, and you were not to deviate from its sage wisdom, no matter what. We know now that's no longer the best practice, unless you've perfected fortune-telling, in which case please give me a call. Otherwise, it's adapt or die for the rest of us.

2. *What you set out to make is not necessarily what you'll end up actually releasing.*

The Lean Startup methodology, which guides entrepreneurs through a series of experiments in the process of starting a business, refers to the shifts in a product's definition as a pivot. We prefer to call these shifts iterations. In both cases, it's a universally accepted truth that great ideas are not great on the first or even the fifth try. Even the most seasoned professionals (including me!!) find that the user often prefers something different from what's expected. It takes a repeated cycle of time, testing, and lots of prototypes to get to the true innovation (or hits).

3. *Putting the product in front of customers is a requirement, not a nice-to-have.*

Steve Blank, author of *The Startup Owner's Manual*, calls it getting out of the office to talk to customers. We call it formative testing of prototypes. In both cases, it means putting things in front of the target audience long before the official launch. It also means *listening* to that audience and addressing its feedback. Use chapter 15 of this book on user testing to help inform the process of collecting feedback.

4. *It's okay to show the audience an unpolished, raw product.*

This is the minimally viable product in startup world or, in other words, the smallest kernel of the product that needs to be built in order to test the idea. It's a prototype, and it shouldn't be something that you've spent years slaving over and perfecting. It's the rough cut. Sometimes it's sloppy, and sometimes it's a taped-together approximation of the idea. But the goal is to create it quickly and inexpensively, yet well enough to get confirmation that you're on the right path. Good enough can actually be good enough!

Are these four things blue-sky thinking? Probably. Is this process right for every project or every client? Definitely not.

Every project is idiosyncratic and hinges on many factors, which means that not all of the conditions described are met. But in an ideal situation, a successful product development cycle starts with an initial game design document, followed by prototyping and testing until you arrive at a product that makes the entire team proud.

In addition to this iterative development mindset, the team must also be well versed in the developmental needs of the target audience (Section Two) as well as in the best practices for game design (Section Three).

Launch the Product

As mentioned in chapter 23, planning for how to launch the product is often an afterthought, but I advocate that planning start early and receive significant attention, including setting aside resources for marketing the product launch. I know it's hard to think about releasing a product when you don't even have the product built. But, with so many products on the market, it's not enough to simply sit back and wait for the magic to happen. You need a plan to rise above the noise. That plan must also include a plan to measure and track your progress against predetermined success metrics.

Parting Thoughts

One thing that's impossible to capture within the pages of a book is the vibrant community of developers in the children's gaming space. It's a very active and passionate group that makes these games. While I'm thrilled you've added *Designing Games for Kids* to your development toolkit, please also make sure you reach out to other developers. Technology changes rapidly, and it's impossible to capture all the nuances and trends in a timely manner. By becoming an active part of the community and engaging in conversation with other designers, you'll gain additional critical insight. We'll continue to raise the bar on children's gaming and entertainment far faster when we're a connected community of designers!

Appendix: Resources for Developers

Children's Developmental Milestones

These resources are great for exploring the average child's developmental path in a number of different ways (e.g., approaches to learning, language, social and emotional growth). Keep in mind that there is a wide range for "normal" when it comes to children; these resources are meant as a guide.

- Babble (www.babble.com/)
- Baby Center (www.babycenter.com/)
- Baby Zone (www.babyzone.com/)
- Disney Family (http://family.go.com/parenting/)
- *Experimenting with Babies: 50 Amazing Science Projects You Can Perform on Your Kid* by Shaun Gallagher (Perigee Books)
- *G Is for Growing: Thirty Years of Research on Children and Sesame Street (Lea's Communications Series)*, edited by Shalom M. Fisch and Rosemarie T. Truglio (Lawrence Erlbaum Associates)
- *How the Child's Mind Develops* by David Cohen (Routledge)
- *Into the Minds of Babes: How Screen Time Affects Children from Birth to Age Five* by Lisa Guernsey (Basic Books)
- Nick Jr.'s Preschool Milestones (www.nickjr.com/preschool/)
- PBS Parents Child Development Tracker (www.pbs.org/parents/child-development/)
- *The Developing Mind: How Relationships and the Brain Interact to Shape Who We Are* by Daniel J. Siegel (Guilford Press)
- *Understanding Comics: The Invisible Art* by Scott McCloud (HarperCollins)

Children's Media Resources

The following list is a mix of resources and information for developers as well as sites that review content for parents and educators.

- Apps Playground (www.appsplayground.com/)
- Children's Online Privacy Protection Act (COPPA) (www.coppa.org/)
- Children's Technology Review (https://childrenstech.com/)
- Common Sense Media (www.commonsensemedia.org/)
- Cynopsis Kids (www.cynopsis.com/editions/kids/)
- Digital Media and Learning Research Hub (DML) (http://dmlhub.net/)
- Edutopia (www.edutopia.org/)

- *Evaluating Children's Interactive Products: Principles and Practices for Interaction Designers* by Panos Markopoulos, Janet C. Read, Stuart MacFarlane, and Johanna Hoysniemi (Morgan Kauffman)
- Fred Rogers Center (www.fredrogerscenter.org/)
- Games and Learning (www.gamesandlearning.org/)
- iKids (http://kidscreen.com/category/ikids/)
- Interaction Design & Children (www.idc-sig.org/)
- iPhone Mom (www.theiphonemom.com/). Find the "For Developers" section for an official review request form and some helpful information.
- Joan Ganz Cooney Center (www.joanganzcooneycenter.org/)
- KAPi's (https://childrenstech.com/kapis)
- Kidscreen (http://kidscreen.com/)
- Media Macaroni (www.mediamacaroni.com/)
- Parents' Choice (www.parents-choice.org/)

Game Design and Business Resources

This is a mix of books and websites with information specific to game design for all ages and types of players as well as resources on business development.

- *A Theory of Fun for Game Design* by Raph Koster (Paraglyph Press)
- App Annie (www.appannie.com/). While this isn't a specific design resource, it is a great tool for researching competitors.
- App Dev Stories (www.appdevstories.com/)
- *Challenges for Game Designers* by Brenda Brathwaite (Cengage Learning)
- ETC Press (http://press.etc.cmu.edu/)
- Gamasutra (www.gamasutra.com/)
- Game Career Guide (www.gamecareerguide.com/)
- Game Developers Conference Vault (www.gdcvault.com/). Not all content is free, but many great talks are.
- Gamesauce (www.gamesauce.org/news/). Gamesauce also hosts all the Casual Connect conference videos.
- GamesBrief.com (www.gamesbrief.com/)
- *The Lean Startup: How Today's Entrepreneurs Use Continuous Innovation to Create Radically Successful Businesses* by Eric Reis (Crown Business)
- *The Multiplayer Classroom: Designing Coursework as a Game* by Lee Sheldon (Cengage Learning)

- *The Startup Owner's Manual: The Step-by-Step Guide for Building a Great Company* by Steve Blank and Bob Dorf (K & S Ranch)
- *Universal Principles of Design, Revised and Updated* by William Lidwell, Kritina Holden, and Jill Butler (Rockport)
- *Well Played Journal* edited by Drew Davidson (ETC Press)

Marketing Resources

The Internet is full of great resources on marketing, but these are some of my favorites.

- *Contagious: Why Things Catch On* by Jonah Berger (Simon & Schuster)
- *Games for a Digital Age: K-12 Market Map and Investment Analysis* by John Richards, Leslie Stebbins, and Kurt Moellering (Joan Ganz Cooney Center)
- *Influence: The Psychology of Persuasion* by Robert Cialdini (Morrow)
- MacWorld (www.macworld.com/)
- *Made to Stick: Why Some Ideas Survive and Others Die* by Chip and Dan Heath (Random House)
- Moz (www.moz.com)
- *Pitch Anything: An Innovative Method for Presenting, Persuading, and Winning the Deal* by Oren Klaff (McGraw-Hill)
- TechCrunch (http://techcrunch.com/)
- *UnMarketing: Stop Marketing. Start Engaging* by Scott Stratten (Wiley)

Conferences

One could spend the entire year jumping from conference to conference. These are some of the recent conferences that have yielded interesting conversations around kids and games.

- App Developers Conference (www.adconf.com/)
- Casual Connect (http://casualconnect.org/)
- Digital Kids Conference (www.digitalkidscon.com/)
- Dust or Magic (www.dustormagic.com/)
- Game Developers Conference (www.gdconf.com/)
- Games for Change Festival (http://gamesforchange.org/festival/)
- Independent Games Festival (www.igf.com/)
- Indie Prize (www.indieprize.org/)
- Interactive Design & Children Conference (www.idc-sig.org/idc-conference/)
- Kidscreen Summit (http://summit.kidscreen.com/)
- Launch Education & Kids Conference (http://edu.launch.co/)
- Sandbox Summit (http://sandboxsummit.org/)

Index

Note: Figures, tables, screenshots and photographs are indicated by italic page numbers.

Printed and bound by CPI Group (UK) Ltd, Croydon, CR0 4YY

22/10/2024

01777642-0004